D1358369

Paint Shop Pro
WEB
Techniques

T. Michael Clark

New Riders Publishing, Indianapolis, Indiana

Paint Shop Pro Web Techniques

By T. Michael Clark

Published by:
New Riders Publishing
201 West 103rd Street
Indianapolis, IN 46290 USA

Printed in the United States of America 1 2 3 4 5 6 7 8 9 0

Library of Congress Cataloging-in-Publication Data

CIP data available upon request

Warning and Disclaimer

This book is designed to provide information about Paint Shop Pro and web graphics. Every effort has been made to make this book as complete and as accurate as possible, but no warranty or fitness is implied.

The information is provided on an "as is" basis. The author(s) and New Riders Publishing shall have neither liability nor responsibility to any person or entity with respect to any loss or damages arising from the information contained in this book or from the use of the disks or programs that may accompany it.

Publisher	*Don Fowley*
Associate Publisher	*David Dwyer*
Marketing Manager	*Mary Foote*
Managing Editor	*Carla Hall*

Senior Acquisitions Editor
John Kane

Development Editor
Jennifer Eberhardt

Technical Editor
Adam Bernstein

Project Editor
Malinda McCain

Copy Editor
Molly Warnes

Senior Editors
Sarah Kearns
Suzanne Snyder

Software Specialist
Steve Flatt

Software Acquisitions
Pete Bitar

Acquisitions Coordinator
Stacey Beheler

Administrative Coordinator
Karen Opal

Cover Designer
Gary Adair

Cover Production
Aren Howell

Book Designer
Sandra Schroeder

Production Manager
Kelly Dobbs

Production Team Supervisors
Laurie Casey
Joe Millay

Graphics Image Specialists
Dan Harris
Debi Bolhuis

Production Analyst
Erich J. Richter

Production Team
Janelle Herber, Linda Knose,
Megan Wade

Indexer
Sandy Henselmeier

About the Author

T. Michael Clark is a Canadian, award-winning web graphics design specialist and an Internet veteran whose lifelong involvement with fine art found a new outlet with the advent of the Information Age. Michael returned to college as a mature student, where he became a computer programmer and software author. While he was in school, Michael's professors constantly urged him to investigate his natural talent for teaching. Readers of his *Powered by GrafX Design* web site agreed, and Michael's first book, *Paint Shop Pro Web Techniques*, is the result. Michael's other interests include portrait and nature photography, cycling, and backpacking in the Adirondacks.

Trademark Acknowledgments

All terms mentioned in this book that are known to be trademarks or service marks have been appropriately capitalized. New Riders Publishing cannot attest to the accuracy of this information. Use of a term in this book should not be regarded as affecting the validity of any trademark or service mark.

Dedications

I'd like to dedicate this book to my beautiful wife, Pamela Clark. Without her help and support throughout every stage of this project, you wouldn't be holding this book in your hands now.

I love you, babe.

Acknowledgments

Okay, where do I start… I feel like it's Oscar night and I'm going to forget somebody.

First, I'd like to thank all the thousands of readers of the GrafX Design web site. If you people hadn't stopped by and encouraged me, I never would have contemplated doing this book. A few names I'd like to mention are some of my earliest and most avid fans: AuntieB, Laren Leonard, Dadoc in Maui (Aloha), all of my Aussie (and there are many) fans—I hope this book makes it all the way there—and all the rest of the people from every corner of the world (some from places I'd never even heard of).

A special thanks goes out to the people at Alien Skin Software, especially Todd Mormon and Michael Pilmer. You guys have restored my faith in the idea that it's possible to do business and still be really cool. All the best.

To my new niece Zoë, who taught me you can be really little and almost helpless and still get your point across if you just try hard enough. I love you, Zoë.

Marianne Dodelet, who generously allowed me to use (and manipulate) her portrait countless times to illustrate the various examples in this book.

My mom, Shirley Clark, who encouraged me to draw at a young age and permitted me to eat supper in front of the TV when any art programs were on. Thanks, Mom!

My mother-in-law, Lillias Walker, for putting up with my incessant discussions of computer networks, the web, computer graphics, and other computer-related topics.

Some of my college science teachers who pestered me constantly about becoming a teacher of some sort, including Mr. Paul Hecht, Dr. Janmohamed, and Dr. G. Saxena. Thanks, guys.

I don't think I can thank the people at New Riders Publishing enough:

John Kane (Senior Acquisitions Editor) and David Dwyer (Associate Publisher) for believing this book *is* a good and timely idea.

John Kane again for getting me over the rough spots in the beginning and for always quickly and patiently answering my panic e-mail. Thanks, John. I look forward to a long and prosperous relationship with you and New Riders.

Jennifer Eberhardt (Development Editor) for being a bigger fan of this project than even me and for being such a big cheering section when I sometimes needed it the most (was that ESP?).

Malinda McCain (Project Editor) who dragged my chapters all the way out to California so she could work on them while visiting her daughter. Now that's commitment.

Adam Bernstein (Technical Editor) for making sure all of the techniques really work. Next to myself, Adam's probably the one person who actually did all of these tutorials.

Stacey Beheler (Acquisitions Coordinator) for all the running around she did to help make sure I got some of the things I needed when I needed them. The shipping people must know her phone voice by heart.

All the rest of the gang at New Riders who were, no doubt, subjected to having to read this book multiple times.

Contents at a Glance

Table of Contents

Introduction

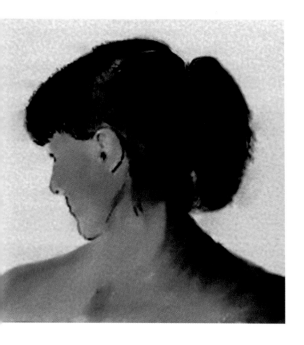

The Birth of *Paint Shop Pro Web Techniques*

Recently, I decided to start up a web design business on the Internet. As I was putting my own site together, I found myself spending more and more time answering user questions on the graphics newsgroups. The way the Internet and the newsgroups in particular work, it seemed that I was frequently answering the same questions. To help cut down on the repetition, I decided to provide a few online web graphics tutorials. I created another site that I called "Powered by GrafX Design" and waited to see what would happen. The response was overwhelming. Some weeks, it took me an entire day to catch up on my e-mail, and it never slowed down. And people have written to me from just about every country you can imagine. You can find "Powered by GrafX Design" at http://www.grafx-design.com.

About a month after I created the GrafX site, I decided that maybe—because the subject seemed so popular—I should write a book. I'd started using Paint Shop Pro (PSP) from JASC Inc. for the online tutorials, even though I use Adobe Photoshop for my own graphical work. It seemed likely that more people could afford the less-expensive Paint Shop Pro. JASC had just released its latest version, with many new features that made it easy to design web graphics. Because there didn't seem to be many books available to walk users through the process of creating computer graphics by using Paint Shop Pro, I decided this topic might be a good idea for a book. What you're holding in your hands is the result of that idea.

Who This Book Is For

If you're interested in creating original, professional-quality graphics for your web site (or anyone else's), this is the book you've been searching for. You don't have to be an artist or know how to see as an artist sees. You may even refer to yourself as "artistically challenged." But even if you can barely draw a stick figure, you'll soon be creating great web graphics if you follow the course this book lays out. From there, whether you're an individual who wants your personal web site to stand out, an amateur webmaster for a special interest group, or a corporate intranet webmaster, the sky's the limit.

Graphics on Your Web Page

The World Wide Web is the graphical portion of the Internet. It's like a combination of a giant magazine and encyclopedia online. It's a newspaper, a catalog, and an information repository. But it isn't so much the information on the web that attracts people to surf online for hours at a time. The web is popular because of the colorful, fun, and interesting ways in which information is presented.

Some of the most successful sites are those that not only carry important and interesting information, but that present the material in a visually pleasing way. I've often bookmarked sites not so much for their written content as for their aesthetics. I often return to those sites to see the fascinating ways in which the designer can grab my attention—and keep me coming back.

Web graphics range from fantastic logos to simple buttons, and from subtle backgrounds to complex and beautiful, yet functional, interfaces. The content of your web site is important

of course, but the layout and visual appeal will keep readers coming back for more.

Original Graphics Versus Clip Art

Now that you've decided to add graphics to your web site, you have a few ways of going about it. You can hire a computer graphic artist—if you have that kind of money. You can buy a CD-ROM full of ready-to-go buttons and backgrounds, set up a site that has a "cloned" look, and then sprinkle it liberally with clip art. If you have this book in your hands, however, that probably means you want to create a look that's uniquely your own—and that's definitely the way to go. You want a site that ties all the content together, one that's tasteful and professional. Even if you've picked up some of the free or shareware clip-art products available on the web, you're probably searching for a way to go even further to spiff up your site and make it stand out.

You don't have to spend hundreds of dollars to put up a clean, professional-looking web site. You probably don't need—or want—to hire a graphics artist for your basic site design. And, you don't have to settle for the prepackaged look. By following this set of tutorials and using the affordable and popular Paint Shop Pro, you'll be able to create your own great-looking graphics for your web page.

Choosing a Graphics Program

There are really only a couple of categories of computer graphics programs. If you plan on becoming a professional web site designer, you might want to investigate all of them thoroughly. I'll describe a couple of the more popular ones to give you an idea of what is available.

Vector-Based Drawing Programs

Vector-based drawing programs, such as Adobe Illustrator and CorelDRAW!, are one option for designing and drawing your web graphics. However, some potential problems are associated with these types of programs. These programs can be more difficult to learn, and they're really designed more for creating artwork that will eventually be printed rather than displayed on a computer monitor. This is not to say you can't use such programs. In fact, I often use CorelDRAW! with a bitmap paint program such as Paint Shop Pro to create interesting interfaces for web sites. But unless you really have the need to create printable graphics, I recommend starting out with a bitmap paint program. After you're used to designing digital graphics, you can always try out a vector-based program if you feel it would be a worthwhile addition to your graphics arsenal.

The graphic shown in figure I.1 was created by using CorelDRAW! A graphic like this would be very hard to create with a bitmap paint program.

Figure I.1

Illustration created with CorelDRAW!

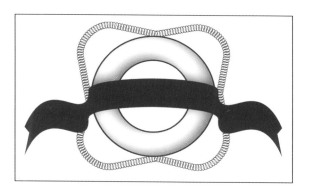

Natural Media Paint Programs

Natural media paint programs are another option worth mentioning. However, before you purchase one, you should be aware that they're meant more for the fine artist. These programs, such as Painter or Sketcher from Fractal Design, let you explore various papers, canvases, and fine art media, and let you create some stunning images.

I created the portrait in figure I.2 by using Painter. The portrait looks as though it were drawn on paper with charcoal when, in fact, the "drawing" in figure 1.2 was done completely on a computer, using a graphics tablet.

Figure I.2

"Pamela" created with Painter.

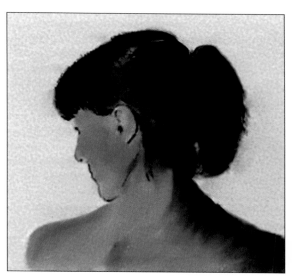

If you're not artistically inclined, you might find this type of software a bit challenging to use. If you discover a hidden talent after designing web pages for a while, however, I highly recommend giving a natural media paint program a try. Who knows—you might be the next Picasso!

3D Rendering Programs

3D programs might not be an obvious choice for creating your web graphics, but programs such as these are gaining in popularity. Webmasters in search of a different look for their pages are finding that 3D graphics can help them achieve this. Previously, the only 3D programs available cost thousands of dollars. Although there are still many high-end rendering programs available, now you can choose from several that cost so little it's worthwhile to buy one just to experiment with computer rendering.

Rendering is a process whereby the computer takes the wireframe of an object, made up of polygons, and applies textures to this frame to "render" a surface. The software also applies light and shadow to the object. These processes are controlled by the artist. It's the artist who decides where in 3D space the object will be placed, what the surface texture will be, where and how many lights will be used, and the opacity of the object. Figure I.3 shows the wireframe preview of a sphere and some 3D text.

At this point, it's difficult to visualize what the final rendering will look like. But because I designed this image and had a specific idea in mind, I had a pretty good idea of what the final graphic would look like. I wanted the letters to be somewhat transparent, and I wanted them to project a shadow onto the sphere. I wanted the sphere to not only have the shadow of the letters on it, but to be somewhat reflective as well. I also chose the colors for all the various visible surfaces. After I made these decisions, and decided how many lights I wanted and what the lights' properties would be, I had the software create the final rendering (see fig. I.4).

Figure I.3

Wire-frame sphere and text created with Simply 3D.

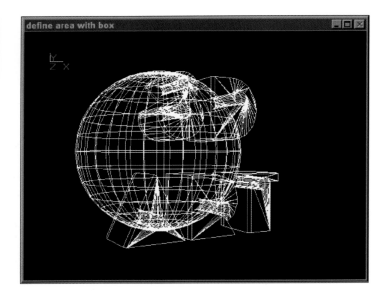

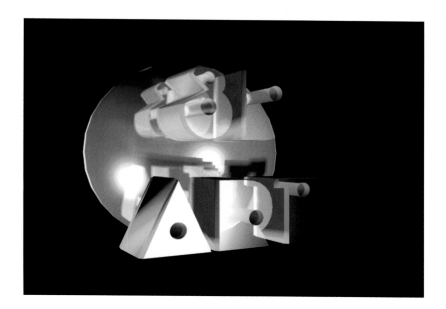

Figure I.4

3D sphere and text created with Simply 3D.

By taking a close look at the final rendering, you can see that I achieved the look I envisioned for this image. When using a program of this type, it's a good idea to have a fairly clear final result in mind and to be able to know how to work toward that idea. The reason for this is that the final rendering can take many hours. I've seen 3D renderings that take almost an entire day to complete. As you become more accustomed to using the 3D program you choose, you'll have more of an idea, when you start a project, of what will be involved in creating the final image.

Although 3D rendering software is nice to have as a second imaging program, I wouldn't recommend it as a first choice for web graphics. Creating all your web graphics with a program like this would take a great deal of time—not to mention the relatively high learning curve involved and the high-end hardware needed to run this type of software.

Because of the calculations involved in computer rendering, there's really no such thing as too much computer power. As a minimum I'd recommend a 486/66 with at least 20 megabytes of RAM. Most graphics programs of this nature also require Microsoft Windows. You'd be better off, in fact, with a higher-end Pentium. As I stated earlier, rendering a complex graphic with several lights can take a whole day's worth of computer time. This is not to say, however, that creating simple 3D text is beyond the reach of the average webmaster.

Bitmap Painting and Photo-Manipulation Programs

These types of programs are best suited for designing web graphics. Everything from the casual title image to some of the most sophisticated web graphics can be designed and created with bitmap paint programs. These programs have the lowest learning curve and, as your skills progress, you'll find that newer and more challenging artwork will become possible without the need to upgrade to more sophisticated drawing programs.

Because of their general imaging qualities, bitmap or paint programs such as Paint Shop Pro and Photoshop are the most widely used type of computer graphics programs for web design. They can be used to manipulate photographs, create web page basics such as buttons, create logos and titles, and even do some illustration. Although paint programs don't have the same flexibility when handling text as illustration programs do, they are capable of producing some stunning results.

Reasons for Choosing Paint Shop Pro

Today, a number of really good bitmap programs are available. And with all of these choices, it's easy to feel bewildered.

Your best bet, however, is Paint Shop Pro from JASC, which is powerful yet fairly easy to use. You can get started with relative ease, and the product will still be able to keep up with you as you become more accustomed to working with digital graphics. Another plus is JASC's marketing approach. JASC has chosen to market its software by using the *shareware* concept. Shareware, contrary to popular belief, isn't a type of software; rather it's a marketing concept. This concept lets you, the user, try out software before spending your hard-earned money on it.

You can obtain a copy of the program by using various methods. You can obtain it directly from JASC's web site, you can download it from many Internet newsgroups and FTP sites, or you can get it from a friend. All these methods are free (or almost free) and perfectly legal. The shareware concept makes this so. Although you can acquire and install the fully functional program on your computer to try it out, you

are legally (and morally) obligated to either purchase the program or stop using it at the end of the trial period.

Note

Paint Shop Pro is available for download from the web site of its creators, JASC Inc, at `http://www.jasc.com`.

The nice part of this is that you can see whether the Paint Shop Pro program meets your needs and whether it runs acceptably on your hardware configuration. If you don't like the program, you don't have to register and pay full price for it. If you find that it gets the job done and want to continue using it, you must call the software company and do the honorable thing by registering the software. After you register, you'll be entitled to certain nice benefits such as low-cost upgrades, a manual, and free technical support. Supporting the shareware concept has the additional benefit of keeping good, cost-effective software on the market (as an alternative to some of the higher-priced professional packages).

As I mentioned previously, other bitmap programs are available. Microsoft Paint, for example, comes free with Microsoft Windows. I know of one online comic strip that's done entirely with MS-Paint. If you want to add some sophistication to your web graphics, however, you'll definitely need more power. At the other end of the spectrum are the programs such as Adobe's Photoshop. This extremely powerful image-editing program has often been referred to as the industry standard. Unfortunately, its high cost prevents it from being the program of choice for most non-graphics professionals. This is where PSP comes in. Although it isn't free, it is inexpensive and has many of the more powerful features you'd expect only in a high-end program such as Photoshop. That, coupled with the "try-before-you-buy" shareware approach, makes Paint Shop Pro an ideal software choice for many webmasters. The cost to register Paint Shop Pro is $69 American, although it can be bought for less online and at some computer stores.

What This Book Will Tell You

Here's a summary section of what you will find in the chapters. As you can see, each chapter builds on the ones before it.

Chapter 1: A Brief Overview of Paint Shop Pro

If you've tried to create your own web graphics, you know some of the problems involved and probably have many questions. Luckily, creating professional-quality web graphics with Paint Shop Pro is relatively painless. Chapter 1 introduces you to this easy to learn, yet powerful paint program.

Chapter 2: Color Quality

Color is one of the hardest things you'll have to deal with when designing web graphics. In Chapter 2, I'll attempt to uncover some of the mysteries surrounding palettes, color depth, and other color-related issues.

Chapter 3: Graphics Quality

Although the choice for file types is still limited when it comes to creating graphics for the World Wide Web, there are many factors to consider. Chapter 3 looks at some of the concerns a Webmaster faces when undertaking the design and creation of web graphics. It also offers some suggestions on how to make the most of what you have to work with.

Chapter 4: Essential Elements of Your Web Page

Chapter 4 covers the essential parts of a web page. I doubt you can find many web pages these days that don't have at least some buttons, bars, or custom bullets. Although I won't be able to show you how to create every type of button, bar, or bullet you can imagine, I'll give you several ideas you can build on.

Chapter 5: Getting Your Message Across

In newsgroups, people often ask how to create a logo for their site. This is a difficult question to answer. I've given the matter some thought, though, and I've decided that the best approach (not to mention one of the easiest) is to stick with using text for logos. Chapter 5 discusses the use of text in the design of logos and web sites.

Chapter 6: Backgrounds and Borders

Backgrounds and borders are a pretty hot topic on the Internet. Ranging from artistic to distracting, backgrounds can help set a particular mood for a web site. Borders have also gained much in popularity. Chapter 6 gives you some examples to try before experimenting to come up with a look that will set your site apart from others.

Chapter 7: Filters

Chapter 7 covers the use of both built-in and third-party filters. Filters can add a lot of functionality to a paint program, making some tasks easier or even enabling you to create certain effects that would be nearly impossible without their use.

Chapter 8: Special Techniques

Chapter 8 reveals a couple of neat tricks you never would have imagined you could pull off with Paint Shop Pro, from transparent GIFs and imagemaps to masks and colorizing black and white photographs. And, even if you never thought you could draw, I'll show you how to turn a photograph into a pencil sketch. Chapter 8 gives all of this and more, using only the options and filters that ship with Paint Shop Pro.

Chapter 9: Putting It All Together

Well, this is it! It's time to take the plunge and put something together. Chapter 9 covers Design Aesthetics, Choosing Your Theme, First Impressions, Following Through, and Using an Effective Interface.

Appendix: Resources on the Internet

This list of resources is not complete by any means but rather a starting point. There are literally thousands of references on the Internet, waiting for you to find them and explore.

Notes, Tips, and Warnings

Paint Shop Pro Web Techniques features many special sidebars, which are set apart from the normal text by icons. This book includes three distinct types of sidebars: Notes, Tips, and Warnings. These sidebars have been given special treatment so you can instantly recognize their significance and easily find them for future reference.

Note

A *note* includes extra information you should find useful. A note might describe special situations that can arise when you use Paint Shop Pro under certain circumstances and might tell you what steps to take when such situations arise. Notes also provide definitions of terms or topics new to the discussion.

Tip

A *tip* provides quick instructions for maximizing your productivity when creating your Paint Shop Pro images. A Tip might show you how to speed up a procedure or how to perform a time-saving or system-enhancing feature.

Warning

A *warning* tells you when a procedure can be dangerous—that is, when you run the risk of a serious problem or error, or even of losing data or crashing your system. Warnings generally tell you how to avoid such problems or describe steps you can take to remedy them.

New Riders Publishing

The staff of New Riders Publishing is committed to bringing you the very best in computer reference material. Each New Riders book is the result of months of work by authors and staff who research and refine the information contained within its covers.

As part of this commitment to you, New Riders invites your input. Please let us know if you enjoy this book, if you have trouble with the information and examples presented, or if you have a suggestion for the next edition.

Please note, however: New Riders staff cannot serve as a technical resource for Paint Shop Pro or for questions about problems related to software or hardware. Please refer to the documentation that accompanies your software or to the applications' Help systems.

If you have a question or comment about any New Riders book, there are several ways to contact New Riders Publishing. We will respond to as many readers as we can. Your name, address, or phone number will never become part of a mailing list or be used for any purpose other than to help us continue to bring you the best books possible.

You can write us at the following address:

New Riders Publishing
Attn: Publisher
201 W. 103rd Street
Indianapolis, IN 46290

If you prefer, you can fax New Riders Publishing at:

317-817-7448

You can also send electronic mail to New Riders at the following Internet address:

jkane@newriders.mcp.com

New Riders Publishing is an imprint of Macmillan Computer Publishing. To obtain a catalog or information, or to purchase any Macmillan Computer Publishing book, call 800-428-5331 or visit our web site at http://www.mcp.com.

Thank you for selecting *Paint Shop Pro Web Techniques*!

Chapter 1

A Brief Overview of Paint Shop Pro

I f you've tried to create your own web graphics, you know some of the problems involved and probably have many questions. Luckily, creating professional-quality web graphics with Paint Shop Pro is relatively painless. This chapter introduces you to this easy to learn, yet powerful paint program:

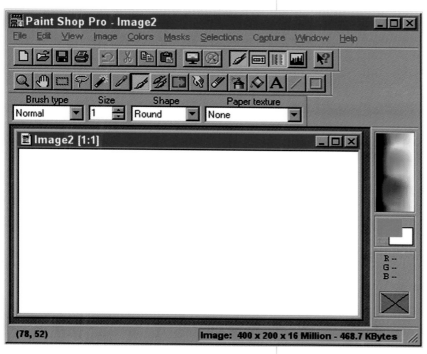

- ▶ Conventions Used in This Book

  - ▶ Mouse Use

  - ▶ Menu Selections

  - ▶ Palettes and Icons

  - ▶ Dialog Boxes

  - ▶ Radio Buttons and Check Boxes

  - ▶ Spin Controls

- ▶ Using Paint Shop Pro

  - ▶ The Menus

  - ▶ The Toolbar

  - ▶ The Tools

  - ▶ The Color Palette

- ▶ Customizing the Interface

Conventions Used in This Book

This book, as every computer tutorial, needs to describe certain actions that you, the user, must perform. Such things as mouse clicks, menu selections, and key presses need to stand apart from the text of the tutorial itself. Because I intend these tutorials to be fairly easy to follow, I'll treat the conventions in the same manner. Instead of using various fonts and styles, I'll keep things as simple as possible.

Mouse Use

If I want you to make a selection by using the mouse, I'll tell you to either click or left-click. This will be the default if you're right-handed. When a right-click is needed, I'll specify right-click. At times I'll also ask you to move the cursor over a certain window, such as the window containing the current image; this is done by using the mouse to position the cursor within that particular window and then left-clicking.

I'll also specify when a double-click is necessary (which happens rarely). When placing the cursor on an image window to make it current, you should only click on the window's title bar or border. Clicking in an inactive window with a tool selected will perform that tool's action.

▌Note

The "current window" to which I'll be referring is simply the image window that should be active for a particular action when there is more than one graphic image open at a time. When this is the case, only one of the windows is "current," while all the others are inactive. The difference is readily apparent—the current window has a Windows 95 "active" color in the title bar and the other(s) have the title displayed in the Windows 95 inactive color. On some systems, for example, the current window has a dark blue title bar and the inactive windows have gray title bars. The colors you see will depend on the settings you have chosen for your Windows 95 setup (see fig. 1.1).

Figure 1.1

Paint Shop Pro windows.

Menu Selections

When I want you to enter a menu selection, I'll describe it like this, where Menu might be File, and Submenu, or command name, might be New:

> Menu, Submenu

If these were File, New, you could follow these instructions to open a new file.

Note

This command means that under one menu selection you'll find others. The second choice will be displayed after you make the first selection from the menu. There might, of course, be more than two choices. In those cases, I'll describe them like this:

> Menu, Submenu, Submenu

Palettes and Icons

If I want you to select a certain tool, I will write, for example, "select the Text tool." This means you should move the mouse over the Text tool icon and click the left mouse button, thereby "selecting" the Text tool.

If a tool is being used for the first time, or if I feel there might be some ambiguity involved in the selection or use of the tool, I'll include a small diagram of its icon.

When it comes to selecting a color from the color swatch, I'll generally provide you with the RGB numbers for that color. However, if I'm describing a general color such as light blue, I might not include the RGB. In those cases I'll expect you to either find a color that's close, or one that suits your purpose.

Note

The meaning and use of RGB is described in Chapter 2, "Color Quality."

Dialog Boxes

I'll refer to the dialog boxes that pop up with certain selections by the names that appear in their title bars. If I feel the information in a dialog box might be a little confusing the first time it's used, I'll show a diagram. Usually, though, I'll just outline the information you need to enter. Often the defaults will be enough, and I'll try to say so when applicable.

Whenever an option needs to be selected—for example, the Antialias option in the Add Text dialog box (see fig. 1.2)—I'll point that out. When an option needs to be turned off, I'll indicate that as well. For example, in figure 1.2 you can see that the Antialias option is checked, or turned on.

Radio Buttons and Check Boxes

Radio buttons are a collection of options of which only one may be selected at a time, and check boxes are a collection of which none, any, or all of the options may be selected.

Radio buttons are round, whereas check boxes are square (see fig. 1.3).

Figure 1.2

Paint Shop Pro Add Text
dialog box.

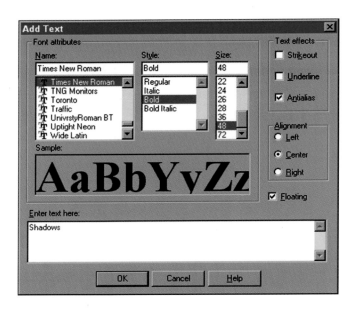

Figure 1.3

Radio buttons and check
boxes as shown in the
Add Text dialog box.

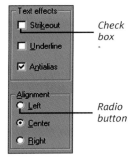

When I've used certain settings on any spin
control—for example, the brightness/contrast
control—I'll describe the settings I used. These
should be regarded as starting points, meaning
I fully expect you to experiment with different
settings. By all means try the settings I've used,
but at the same time feel free to make adjustments and see how the results differ. It's only
through this type of exercise that you'll fully
appreciate the capabilities of Paint Shop Pro.

Spin Controls

Spin controls like the one shown in figure 1.4
enable you to enter integer values. The range
permitted depends on the option for which the
spin control is activated. The value within that
range can be raised and lowered by clicking on
the small arrows to the right of the number. To
save time, though, a number can also be
entered directly into the small window to the
left of the arrows after selecting the field with
the mouse.

Figure 1.4

Spin control

Using Paint Shop Pro

If you're already familiar with Paint Shop Pro,
feel free to skip this quick review and move on
to Chapter 2.

Figure 1.5 shows what the Paint Shop Pro 4.0 window looks like when you start the program. If you're using the shareware version, the window indicates which day of your 30-day free trial you're on and suggests that you register.

Remember, if you find that Paint Shop Pro gets the job done and want to continue using it, you must call the software company and do the honorable thing by registering the software. After you register, you'll be entitled to certain fringe benefits such as low-cost upgrades, a manual, and free technical support. Supporting the shareware concept has the additional benefit of keeping good, cost-effective software on the market (as an alternative to some of the higher-priced professional packages).

The Menus

At the top of the screen you'll see the menu bar (see fig. 1.6). From the menu bar you can select different functions and the options associated with these functions.

The **File menu** enables you to Open, Close, Save, Save As, and so on. More important, this is where you set your program preferences. For example, this is where you can set up the plug-in filters directory. At the bottom of this menu choice, you'll see a list of the most recent files you've worked on. This can be a very useful timesaver—you can just click on the name of a file in this list rather than using the Open File dialog box. Batch processing of graphics files is done from the file menu as well. This will be discussed in Chapter 3, "Graphics Quality."

Menus

Function bar

Options for currently active tool

Current X, Y coordinates of cursor

Figure 1.5

Tools palette

Color palette

Current file information

Figure 1.6

Paint Shop Pro menu bar.

File   Edit   View   Image   Colors   Masks   Selections   Capture   Window   Help

The **Edit menu** contains editing functions such as Undo, Cut, Paste, and Clear. The paste function has several options that will be discussed as we go through the tutorials in later chapters.

The **View menu** enables you to change the way you view the current image. For example, you can view a Full Screen Preview, or you can zoom in and out. You can see the image through its mask if one is active, and you can also turn on and off the various "palettes."

The **Image menu** holds the most menu functions, and exploring its capabilities is very worthwhile. From this option, you can Resample, Resize, and Rotate the image. You can also choose from among the special effects, built-in filters, and available plug-ins. Many functions accessible from the Image menu offer a set of options or a submenu.

The **Colors menu** enables you to manipulate the colors of your graphic. Some of the options offered in this menu are Grayscale, Colorize, and Posterize. This is where you can load, save, and edit color palettes. Also, you can adjust the color resolution by setting the number of colors in your graphic.

The **Masks menu** enables you to create, edit, save, and load *masks*. This very powerful feature can be helpful for applying selective effects such as Blurring, Brightening, and Darkening to different images or portions of images.

The **Selections menu** also offers a powerful set of tools and now contains features that used to be available only with high-end paint programs. You can make selections, deselect, or invert a selection. You can also save and load selections.

In Chapter 8, "Special Techniques," I'll show how you can even draw by using these powerful tools. You can modify your selections from the Selections menu, as well.

The **Capture menu** enables you to set up and use the screen capture function.

The **Window menu** is your standard MS-Windows menu choice. It enables you to Cascade, Tile, and Duplicate windows.

Last, but not least, is the **Help menu**, which, of course, runs the Paint Shop Pro 4.0 online help.

Some of these functions are also available on the Functions icon bar, described briefly in the next section, which you can customize to meet your needs.

The Toolbar

Figure 1.7 shows (in groups from the left) the toolbar. You can turn it on or off in the View menu.

▶ The File functions: New, Open, Save, and Print

▶ The Editing functions: Undo, Cut, Copy, and Paste

▶ The Full-Screen Preview and Normal Viewing icons

▶ A group that toggles off and on the other palettes: the Tool palette, Style bar, Color palette, and Histogram

The icon at the far right is, of course, the Help icon.

The Tools

Below the toolbar is the Tools palette (see fig. 1.8). You can turn it on or off in the View menu.

The first icon on the left is the **Zoom tool**, which is used to change the view of the current image. Left-clicking on the image while this tool is active zooms in, and right-clicking on the image zooms out. This can be useful for getting in close and making very small changes and selections in a graphic.

The **Hand tool** moves an image around within the image window if the image is too large to be seen in the current image window. If you see scroll bars along the bottom and/or right side of the image window, the image is too big for the current window.

The next three icons are the Selection tools. **Selection** (the dotted rectangle) enables you to make circular, elliptical, square, and rectangular selections. The **Lasso** makes freehand selections, and the **Magic Wand** selects areas of a graphic based on the color. All these tools have options that will change the way they behave. These options appear in a style bar below the Tool palette after you select the tool. You can also *add to* and *subtract from* selections—another powerful feature of Paint Shop Pro 4.0.

When you click on the mouse buttons, the **Eyedropper tool** changes the foreground (left button) or background (right button) color to the color you've selected in the current graphic.

The **Brush tool** enables you to draw and paint with various brushes and pens, all of which have some very useful options. As you progress through the tutorials in the book, you'll learn more about these options.

The icon with the double brush is the **Cloning brush**. It's very helpful for photo retouching and cleaning up areas of a graphic. It can also be used to help make the necessary adjustments

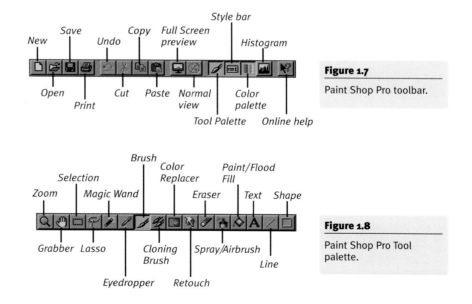

Figure 1.7

Paint Shop Pro toolbar.

Figure 1.8

Paint Shop Pro Tool palette.

when creating seamless tiles. The blue and red icon is the **Color Replacer tool**. This is used to replace all instances of one particular color in your image with another. After you set the colors, using the foreground/background color swatch, you can change the color throughout the whole image with just two clicks of the mouse. Double-click the left mouse button anywhere on the image to replace the background color (on the swatch) with the foreground color. Double-click the right mouse button to perform the reverse process.

The icon picturing the pointing finger is the **Retouch tool**. This is used to lighten, darken, sharpen, smudge, and even emboss parts of your graphic.

The **Eraser tool** is less an eraser and more a selective *undo*. You can use this tool to selectively undo parts of the most recent change you've made.

The **Spray (airbrush) tool** is not only useful for adjusting images and photos, but can also be used as a drawing tool, as we'll see in the graffiti tutorial in Chapter 5, "Getting Your Message Across."

The **Paint (flood fill)** tool enables you to fill areas with solid colors, gradients, and patterns.

The **Text tool** is used to add text to your graphics, using any font you have available on your system. This tool enables you to antialias your text if you're in 16.7 million colors mode. You can also adjust the opacity of the text, as well as perform other cool tricks, which you'll see in the tutorials.

The **Line tool** enables you to draw straight lines of varying thicknesses.

Last, the **Shape tool** is used to draw outlined or filled circles, ellipses, squares, and rectangles.

Depending on which tool is currently active, you'll also see a style bar that enables you to select from among the various options, or styles, available for the current tool.

Figure 1.9 shows what you will see if the active tool is the Brush, for example. Here you can adjust the brush type, size, and shape, and select a paper texture if you wish to do so.

Figure 1.9

Paint Shop Pro style bar.

The Color Palette

To the right of the main Paint Shop Pro window is the Color palette (see fig. 1.10). Here you'll find the Color Picker and the current foreground/background swatch. You'll also see the RGB numbers listed, along with a swatch (the gray square with the black cross in this diagram). The RGB number shows you which color you're over if the cursor—which changes to the Eyedropper tool when you're on the Color Picker—is over the image.

Figure 1.10

Paint Shop Pro Color palette.

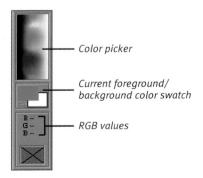

Color picker

Current foreground/ background color swatch

RGB values

This is much easier to see than it is to explain. To get a better idea of what I'm talking about, you'll need to move the mouse over the multi-colored area in the palette. Then you'll see the gray-colored swatch change color as you do so. Also, you'll see the RGB values change to reflect the color the mouse is located over.

Although it is not highly accurate, moving the mouse over the Color Picker is a quick way to approximate the color you want. At this point, clicking on the color swatch sets the foreground (left-click) or background (right-click) color. Clicking on either the foreground or background color swatch brings up the Color dialog box. You can further fine-tune the color you've chosen by changing the shade of the color, or you can even change the color altogether by entering a new set of RGB values. RGB and color selection will be discussed further in Chapter 2.

The large gray area of the screen is the work area. This is where you'll see the images you're working on. In figure 1.11 you can see a new file open with no image drawn on it yet. In the title bar of the image is its name (in this case, Image2) and its current zoom level (in this case [1:1], meaning it is shown at its normal size).

At the very bottom of the screen is the current file information.

At the bottom right of the screen you'll see the image size in pixels, the color resolution, and the file size in bytes. At the left of this area is a very important bit of information. The two numbers in the parentheses indicate the current X and Y coordinates of the cursor within the graphic. This information is very helpful when drawing, selecting, and moving areas of your graphic, because it tells you where you are on the graphic.

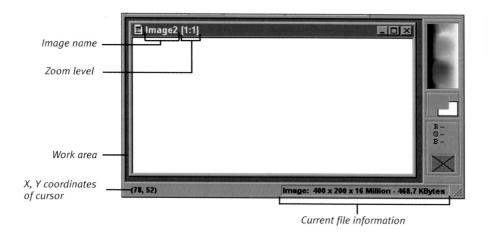

Figure 1.11

Paint Shop Pro status bar.

Image name

Zoom level

Work area

X, Y coordinates of cursor

Current file information

Customizing the Interface

The Paint Shop Pro 4.0 interface can be customized to a certain degree. If, for example, you're doing a lot of scanning, you can set up a button to acquire an image and another to gamma-correct it. These customizations can be set up by choosing File, Preferences, Customize, which will give you a dialog box full of icons. If you find yourself constantly repeating the same task from the menu, you can check here to see if there is an icon you can set up to perform the task instead. For example, if you are engaged in scanning in and gamma-correcting a number of photographs, you could save yourself some time by adding the Scanning and Gamma-Correction icons to your toolbar.

▌Definition

Gamma refers to a computer monitor's brightness and contrast. After an image has been scanned into the computer, you can adjust the image's gamma. This combines the brightness and contrast adjustments and is much easier to apply.

Summary

Although this chapter was really a very brief overview, I've tried to include most of the information you need to get started. Paint Shop Pro is fairly easy to use—when you roll up your sleeves and get started, you'll be surprised at how quickly you pick up the skills required to start creating your own web graphics.

If you've used previous versions of Paint Shop Pro, you've probably noticed some of the new features in Paint Shop Pro 4.0. These new features are mostly geared to web graphics creation. In addition, some of the existing tools, such as the Selection tools, have been upgraded and now include features previously available only in high-end graphics programs.

Whether you're just starting out as a web designer or are a seasoned professional, you'll find Paint Shop Pro will fit your design needs quite nicely.

The next section of the book deals with color, how it relates to web graphics, and how it can be used in Paint Shop Pro. There are a lot of pitfalls when it comes to screen-based graphics and color, but Chapter 2 will show how they can be overcome.

Chapter 2

Color Quality

Color quality is something all designers of web graphics must be concerned with. You've probably heard about the "browser-safe palette" and might be wondering how it would affect the display of your images. You might also wonder why you can't just create your images at one color depth or another, or why some options are grayed out when you want to select them.

Color is one of the hardest things you'll have to deal with when designing web graphics. In this chapter, I'll attempt to uncover some of the mysteries surrounding palettes, color depth, and other color-related issues.

▶ The Use of Color

    ▶ Color in Paint Shop Pro

    ▶ Palettes in Paint Shop Pro

    ▶ Understanding Color Depth

    ▶ Working with Grayscale

    ▶ Understanding RGB

    ▶ Using Hue, Saturation, and Luminance

▶ Color on the Web

    ▶ Choosing the Right Colors

    ▶ Adding Contrast

    ▶ Dithering Your Graphics

    ▶ The Netscape Palette

The Use of Color

Colors play an important role in our lives. We often use colors as visual cues. Traffic lights, for example, provide information to us based on the color they display—red for stop, green for go, and yellow for caution.

It has also been shown that colors can have a profound effect on our emotions. Bright, vivid colors cause our heart rates to elevate, and sub-dued pastel colors can actually have a calming effect. Certain colors also have traditional meanings—for example, in some cultures red represents passion and white represents purity or innocence. An abstract painting that uses pri-marily red invokes a different response in view-ers than does one that uses shades of blue. The knowledge of how colors affect people can be of use to an artist, and a webmaster who uses color appropriately on a web site can influence the feelings of people who view its pages.

Note

For a full description of color use on the World Wide Web, see *Coloring Web Graphics* by Lynda Weinman and Bruce Heavin.

As an example, though, look at the imagemap in figure 2.1.

As you look at the page, notice how your eye keeps being drawn to the GrafX logo; in fact, you probably notice it before anything else. This happens because of the red lettering. The natural progression your eye follows from there is to the word "tips," partly because we read from left to right and from top to bottom, but also because of the contrast between the lighter part of the silver background and the word itself.

Figure 2.1

GrafX Design imagemap.

The logo is the most visible part of the graphic, as intended. The next part you see should be the title or heading. You will note that even though the word "tips" is not very prominent, your eye comes to rest on it frequently as you look over the whole image. From there your eye naturally moves down the line of buttons.

Perhaps you also noticed that although the presence of the round icons at the left of the image is evident, your eyes are not distracted by them. This is due in part to their softer pastel colors. The buttons are there and you see them, but they're not intrusive. This imagemap is not only functional but gets its purpose across in a way that is not immediately obvious, partially due to the colors used.

Color on the web can have other meanings as well. If you're a regular web surfer, you proba-bly recall, for example, when a lot of webmas-ters used black backgrounds on their web pages to support a massive protest against limiting freedom of speech on the web and the Internet.

Life would be pretty dull if everything appeared in black and white. Fortunately, humans are capable of seeing the world in a wide array of colors. Given the length of the spectrum of light, the number of colors we see is somewhat limited, but all things considered, we can perceive a large number of colors.

When it comes to using color on our computers, though, the limitation isn't necessarily how many colors your system can display. Even with a state-of-the-art video card and monitor that are capable of displaying almost 17 million colors, a web page designer can still encounter problems. The reason for the problems, most notably the "jaggies," is more a function of the resolution of the monitor than of how many colors it can display. The typical PC computer screen displays only 640×480 pixels, and with only that many pixels-worth of information, some limitations are to be expected.

To illustrate these limitations, figure 2.2 shows a black oval on a white background.

You don't need to zoom in to see how jagged this oval appears. Most webmasters would rather not put something like this up on their site. So what can be done? There are a number of solutions available. Some involve using different color combinations, and others involve using some form of what is known as *antialiasing*.

Figure 2.3 illustrates the use of color combinations to help eliminate the appearance of "jaggies." For example, if a light gray color is used for the oval, it appears less jagged.

It's not a lot better, but it is better. The oval now looks less jagged because of the way our eyes (and our brains, really) process information. The light gray shade is much more similar to the white than the black shade was, causing your brain to see less of an edge and more of a blending of the gray and the white.

Choosing the colors for web graphics with these limitations in mind can improve how the images appear on a computer screen.

Another limiting factor is the number of colors that can be displayed. Not all computer users

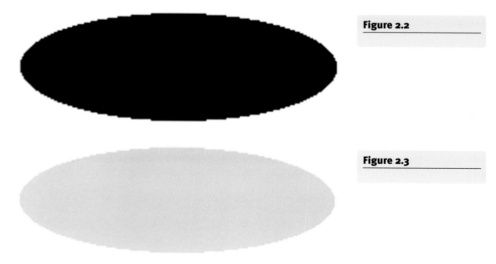

Figure 2.2

Figure 2.3

have the hardware necessary to display 16.7 million or even 64,000 colors. Many web surfers actually view web pages while using only 256 colors. (I've even heard of some who surf with a computer that can only display 16 colors, yikes!) How does that affect webmasters who use Paint Shop Pro to design their web graphics, and which 256 colors should they use? Paint Shop Pro uses *color palettes*, ranges of colors specific to individual images. I'll examine how palettes are used in Paint Shop Pro a little further on and discuss how to deal with what has come to be known as "the Netscape palette" in the "Colors on the Web" section.

Color in Paint Shop Pro

When using Paint Shop Pro, you can create and modify images containing from 2 to 16.7 million colors. When you're using the 16.7 (or 24-bit) mode—I always suggest starting with this—you can select colors by using the Color dialog box (see fig. 2.4).

This dialog box appears if you left-click on either the foreground or background color swatch. The large multi-colored square is the Color Picker area. You can click anywhere within this area to change or "pick" a new color. To the right of the Color Picker area is a slider you can use to change the shade of the current color. Below the picker and slider are a couple of windows. The largest displays the current color, which in figure 2.4 is white, while the smaller windows (those with the numbers in them) let you manually set the HSL (hue, saturation, luminance) or RGB (red, green, blue) numbers for a particular color. At the very bottom is the Add to Custom Colors button that enables you to add the current color you've selected to a set of custom colors. On the left side of the Color dialog box is a set of standard colors and an area in which you can store up to 16 custom colors. If you are working on an image that contains fewer than 16.7 million colors (for example, 256 or 16 colors), you will be working with what is called a *palette*.

Figure 2.4

Paint Shop Pro's Color dialog box.

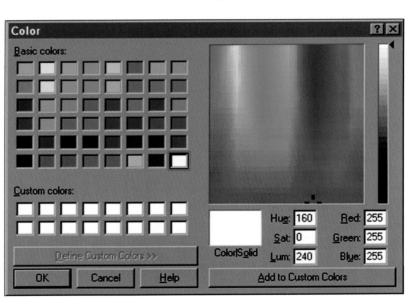

Palettes in Paint Shop Pro

Paint Shop Pro has the ability to save and load what are known as color palettes. Each palette contains a certain number of colors, depending on the color depth of the current image, which the designer can use while editing the image. Clicking on either the foreground or background color swatch while working on a limited color image will bring up the Edit Palette dialog box instead of the Color dialog box. Palettes can be either created or downloaded. Also, any graphic loaded into Paint Shop Pro that has a limited color depth, such as a GIF file, will contain its own color palette. For example, the imagemap shown in figure 2.5 has mostly copper tones.

Let's take a look at this graphic's color palette (see fig. 2.6). You can open it by clicking on either the foreground or background color swatch.

Figure 2.5

Sample copper-colored imagemap.

After you load this image, you can use its palette to create other images with the same range of colors. Of course, the ideal situation is

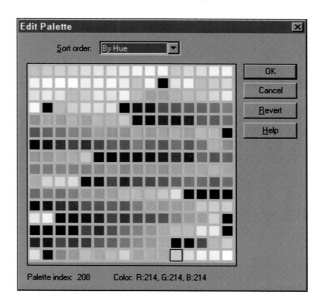

Figure 2.6

Copper colors palette.

being able to choose from 16.7 million colors. In fact, as you'll see later, this is the only color depth that gives you full control over Paint Shop Pro and all the effects it can create.

Understanding Color Depth

What exactly is color depth, and how does it affect the graphics you create for your web pages? To understand the answer to these questions, you'll have to bear with me through a little computer arithmetic. I promise to make it as painless as possible.

By now, most people are familiar with the terms "*bits*" and "*bytes*." Most people also know that 8 bits make up a byte, right? What you might not know is that a bit is the smallest piece of information a computer can process. A bit can have two states, on or off, sometimes described as 1 or 0, respectively. It's because of this bit and byte business that computer arithmetic looks a little funny to us humans. We think of numbers in terms of decimal values, because we have 10 (or *deca*) fingers (and 10 toes, for that matter). Computers, seeing things as they do in terms of on and off, do their arithmetic in binary (*bi* as in two). Because bits are generally grouped together eight at a time, computer numbers are described as 8-bit, 16-bit, 24-bit, 32-bit, and so on, all divisible by 8.

To illustrate how this works, here's a little computer arithmetic:

How many colors can you display with 8 bits? The answer is 2^8, or 256 colors. That is the amount of information a bit can hold—**2**—to the power of the number of bits—**8**. Here's another example:

What if you had a 24-bit video card? Then you could display 2^{24}, or 16,777,216 colors. Does this number look familiar? You will see numbers like these (256 colors, 16.7 million colors) in the pull-down menu that appears when you select Decrease Color Depth or Increase Color Depth from the Colors menu. This is known as *color depth*, that is, how many bits-worth of color your hardware is capable of displaying. The importance of this will become more apparent in parts of Chapter 3, "Graphics Quality," Chapter 7, "Filters," and in Chapter 8, "Special Techniques," (for example, when I discuss antialiasing).

Working with Grayscale

Although we've been discussing the importance and use of color versus black and white, black and white does have its place in graphic art. Black and white images—or grayscale images as they're known in computer-speak—can be used to add drama to your web graphics. When using grayscale, you are limited to 256 shades of gray, ranging from white through the various shades of gray to black. The reason for the 256 shades of gray is, again, partly due to the way computers deal with numbers and arithmetic and partly to how the screen, or video card, displays colors. When using grayscale you might notice that the values in the "RGB" settings are always equal. What I mean by this is that an RGB value of *0, 0, 0* represents the color black, the RGB value *255, 255, 255* is white, and the RGB value *128, 128, 128* is a medium gray. In other words, anytime you select a shade of gray, the R value, the G value, and the B value will all be the same. Because this is true, there can only be 256 gray shades, from 0, 0, 0 through 255, 255, 255.

Understanding RGB

There are two different descriptions of color you'll come across as you design web graphics with Paint Shop Pro, the most common of which is RGB. RGB stands for Red, Green, and Blue. By using a value between 0 and 255 for each of these three colors, you can display 16.7 million colors. To illustrate this, we can figure out the available possibilities. If we go from 0, 0, 0 to 255, 255, 255, there are, indeed, 256×256×256, or 16,777,216 colors. Because each of the numbers from 0 to 255 can be represented with one byte (or 8 bits), and we have three bytes (24 bits) available, this explains today's 24-bit video card. Expressed another way, $2^8 \times 2^8 \times 2^8 = 256 \times 256 \times 256 = 16,777,216$. That wasn't so bad, right?

Note

Other ways of describing colors, such as CMYK (Cyan, Magenta, Yellow, and percentage of Black), are used when printing colors on paper. This will not be of immediate concern to most webmasters, however, because the images they create will generally be viewed on the computer screen.

Using Hue, Saturation, and Luminance

Another way of expressing color is HSL, which stands for Hue, Saturation, and Luminance. Using this method, you again have numbers ranging from 0 to 255. This time, though, you use the values to express hue (color), saturation (amount of color), and luminance (brightness of the color). I'll look at this a little more when you start playing with colorization and with brightness and contrast. Just to add a little confusion, HSL is sometimes written as HSB, with the B standing for brightness instead of luminance. Same thing, different terminology.

Color on the Web

Given all I've discussed in the preceding section, you can start to see how important color choice is when designing web graphics. There are a lot of factors to consider if you want your images to convey a message or a certain feeling. There's even more to be concerned about if you want your images to appear with the best possible quality.

Choosing the Right Colors

I'm not going to discuss which colors go best with others here. However, the one thing you'll find me repeating over and over when I start a tutorial is this: Choose a background color that comes closest to the background color you'll be placing your graphics against. This is really only important if you'll be designing an image with a transparent background so it can be placed on a web page that has a background pattern, or if you'll be designing, for example, text or a logo with drop shadows. Instead of trying to explain what will happen, I'll show you a couple of examples that will give you a much better idea of the need for setting the appropriate background color.

First, look at what happens when you design an image with a drop shadow set on a blue background and then place the image on a page with a white background.

Here's the image as it was designed (see fig. 2.7).

Figure 2.7

Okay, maybe it doesn't contain the best combination of colors overall, but it doesn't look too bad. Now I'll show you what happens when I set the background color to transparent and place this image on a white background (see fig. 2.8).

Figure 2.8

Yuck! Notice the blue outlines around the text and the drop shadow? I'll explain why this happens after showing you one more example.

You probably won't run into this kind of problem as often as you will the next one. Most people don't start off a graphic with a blue background; in fact, Paint Shop Pro typically defaults to a white background. This means you'll usually design your image with a white background, set the white as transparent, if necessary, and then load the graphic onto your page. Figure 2.9 shows how the graphic might look after you first design it.

Figure 2.9

Pretty nice. The red text on the white background is quite striking. In fact, the drop shadow makes the text stand out even more. What happens, though, if I move this image to a page with a blue background? Check out figure 2.10.

Figure 2.10

Yikes! That's even worse than the last example.

The outline around the text and drop shadows in these examples is a result of antialiasing. To help smooth out the image, Paint Shop Pro uses a little arithmetic to choose colors that lie between the foreground and background colors, and then uses pixels of those colors to blend the edges of the text or shadow into the background. The eye is fooled into thinking the image is not jagged. I'll take a closer look at this subject in the section on antialiasing in Chapter 3.

Of course, this problem is fairly easy to deal with if you're going to place the text image against a solid background, but what if you intend to place it against a patterned background? In that case I'd recommend using a color that closely matches the color that occurs most frequently in the pattern you have selected.

Figure 2.11 shows a perfect example of the type of difficulty you might encounter. The easiest solution, of course, would be to create the text and its shadow directly on the background image. Unfortunately, the way web browsers display backgrounds and images doesn't allow you this luxury. (HTML won't allow specific placement of images.) You could just place the text on a copy of the background graphic; however, the chances of this lining up with the background on the web page are slim at best, resulting in a truly unprofessional-looking web site.

An image such as the one in figure 2.11 contains so many shades of green you might have some trouble settling on an optimal shade for the background. I had to make a couple of attempts to get this one right. At first I set the text against a light green chosen from the background pattern. It didn't work out too well, though, and the light green outline was too visible. I then decided a darker green might work better. You can still see some of the outline around the bottom of the drop shadow on the *S* and the *h*, but overall it's not bad. This just

goes to show that even an experienced graphic artist needs to work at achieving the desired result.

Adding Contrast

As you saw with the black oval and the gray oval (see figs. 2.2 and 2.3), the designer's choice of colors can have an effect on the apparent quality of the image. The gray oval looked better because the gray color contrasted less with the white background than the black color did. This is good news, because if you really want the oval to be black, all you need to do is place it against a background that has a low level of contrast with the black. Placing the black oval on a shade of blue, perhaps, would give the desired effect, so although the choices are somewhat limited, the situation is not altogether hopeless. Later I'll show you other options that will actually enable you to place that black oval on the white background and still have an acceptable level of jaggedness.

Dithering Your Graphics

Dithering is what happens when a system displays a graphic that contains more colors than the system is capable of displaying—that is,

Figure 2.11

Drop-shadowed text on textured background.

when you try to view a 16.7 million color graphic with a display capable of showing only 256 colors. Dithering is accomplished by using one of several mathematical algorithms.

Essentially what happens is that the system tries to fake the needed color by combining some of the available colors in different patterns. Sometimes this works out well and other times it looks pretty bad. Pretend you have a system only capable of displaying black and white, and what you need is a shade of gray. The computer might fake the gray color by using repeating lines of black and white, as shown in figure 2.12.

Figure 2.12

Hand-dithered gray, using lines of black and white.

Or say you need a purple color that isn't available on a particular system. It might be approximated by using lines of red and blue (see fig. 2.13).

Figure 2.13

Hand-dithered purple, using red and blue.

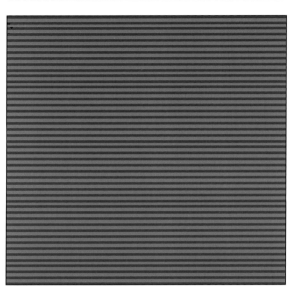

The dithering algorithms make use of mathematical formulas. These do a more complicated and much better job of displaying "unavailable" colors than the repeating line method, of course, but the idea is basically the same. Through the use of dithering, the system can use only the colors that are available, yet fool the human eye into believing there are more colors than those actually present in a limited palette.

The Netscape Palette

Let's say you've just spent a couple of hours designing some spiffy graphics for your web page, and they look great! You upload the changes to your Internet server, fire up Netscape, and HORRORS! The graphics don't look at all like the ones you spent hours working on. What's the story?

This is a kind of complicated, nerdy topic, but you need to know what's going on, so I'll try to work you through it with as little pain as possible.

If you or the people who view your web pages do so on a system that displays only 256 colors, you have a problem. Even if you design your graphics on a 256-color system, chances are they'll appear different when viewed with Netscape.

The problem lies in the fact that even though the system only displays 256 colors, it can choose those colors from among 16.7 million. You've probably viewed a black-and-white photo on your system, right? Well, that photo was probably displayed with 256 shades (or colors, if you will) of gray, so even though you're only seeing 256 colors, you're seeing a different set of 256 colors than were used when the photo was scanned into the computer.

You might have noticed, however, that some of the grays in the photo you saw weren't really gray. They might have been a pale shade of red, blue, or green. This happens because the system can only choose 256 colors, and some colors are actually needed by the system itself (we're talking Windows here). The same can be said of

Netscape; it retains some colors for its own use. In fact, Netscape and Windows together use 40 of the 256 colors available on an 8-bit system. This actually leaves 216 colors for a web page designer's use. You might hear this palette referred to as the "cube," a 6×6×6 set (6×6×6 = 216) of colors Netscape will use without dithering. They're also considered "browser-safe" colors.

If a system is limited to 256 colors, the software displaying an image—in this case Netscape—decides which 256 colors to use. If you take this into account when you're designing your graphics, you won't have to worry about how your images will display on various viewers' systems. All your graphics will appear the same on any machine that displays your web pages by using Netscape, whether those systems are running with 256 colors or 16.7 million colors.

So how do you know which colors are safe to use and which aren't? Simple! You can visit the JASC web site at http://www.JASC.com and pick up the Netscape palette. If you use this palette when designing your web graphics, you shouldn't have any problems.

After you download the "zipped" palette file, you can unzip it to the Paint Shop Pro directory on your hard drive. You can then set up Paint Shop Pro to use it by choosing Colors, Load Palette to bring up a dialog box where you can tell the program where the palette is.

After you have designated the Netscape palette, you can see the available colors by clicking on either the foreground color swatch or the background color swatch. This brings up the "Edit Palette" dialog box as shown in figure 2.14.

Figure 2.14

Edit Palette dialog box.

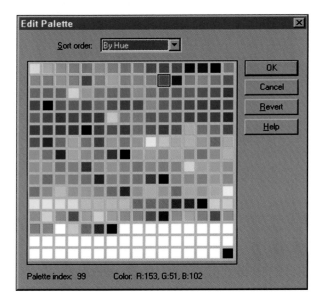

Make sure you don't change any of these colors!

"Okay," you say, "but what if I've already created a graphic and need to be sure it'll use the Netscape colors?"

Easy (well, sort of): Load the graphic and, while still in Paint Shop Pro, load the Netscape palette. This will dither all the colors to the ones available in the palette. If at this point your graphic looks really different, you've got some work to do.

Figure 2.15 shows a popular button from the Powered by GrafX Design web site. Believe it or not, this button contains 3033 colors.

Figure 2.15

About Button in 16.7 million colors.

After I load the Netscape palette, the button's appearance undergoes a radical change (see fig. 2.16).

Figure 2.16

About Button with Netscape palette applied.

Not too pretty, eh? Only 52 colors, a little muddy, and some pretty bad dithering.

Figure 2.17 shows what the button looks like after a little tweaking with the Paint tool and Pen tool and a few color selections from the Netscape palette.

It took some work and still isn't as nice as the 3033-color graphic, but it's certainly much nicer than the dithered one. The button still has that reflective gold look, and the text is less muddy. Now, I'm also sure this is how it will appear to virtually everyone who views it (no pun intended).

You might have to get used to doing this, because when you are creating a graphic, I'll usually have you start out with 16.7 million colors. The higher color resolution is necessary in order to use all the functions Paint Shop Pro provides. If you later decide to change an image's colors to those of the Netscape palette, you'll either have to roll up your sleeves and do a little pixel editing or hope your graphics are seen by users with systems powerful enough to view many colors. Either way, the choice is up to you.

At least now you know why dithering happens when you change an image's palette to the Netscape palette, and how you can have some control over the result.

Where does this leave you as a web graphics designer? This is a decision only you can make. You should design your graphics at a high color resolution, though, to take advantage of the features available at this resolution. If you're really concerned about how your graphics will appear, you can always roll up your sleeves, apply the Netscape palette, and do some pixel editing.

Chapter 3

Graphics Quality

Although the choice for file types is still limited when it comes to creating graphics for the World Wide Web, there are many factors to consider. This chapter will look at some of the concerns a webmaster faces when undertaking the design and creation of web graphics. It'll also offer some suggestions on how to make the most of what you have to work with. The following topics will be covered:

- ▶ Using Paint Shop Pro-Compatible File Types

    - ▶ Web-Specific File Types

    - ▶ GIF

    - ▶ JPG

    - ▶ PNG

- ▶ Converting and Manipulating Graphics Files

    - ▶ Batch Conversion

    - ▶ Resizing and Resampling

    - ▶ Cropping and Enlarging

    - ▶ Antialiasing

- ▶ Feathering

- ▶ GIF or JPG?

- ▶ Lossy Versus Lossless Compression

- ▶ Compression and Color Depth

- ▶ Transparent GIFs

- ▶ Interlaced GIFs and Progressive JPGs

Using Paint Shop Pro-Compatible File Types

Paint Shop Pro 4.0 can load, save, and convert between 35 different file formats, 26 raster (or bitmap) types, and nine meta and vector-based types. Of course, not all these file types can be used on the web. Sometimes the image file you've been searching for is only available in TIF, BMP, or TGA, which are all non-web–compatible formats. No problem! Paint Shop Pro 4.0 can convert these files to JPG or GIF so you can use them on your web site. Even better, if you have a number of these conversions to do, Paint Shop Pro 4.0 will do them in batch. This means that rather than loading, converting, and re-saving each file one by one, Paint Shop Pro 4.0 enables you to specify a bunch of conversions and then takes care of them for you automatically. The method for batch conversion is fairly simple and is discussed further on in this chapter.

If you use a vector-based program such as CorelDRAW! or Adobe Illustrator, you can create your graphic in one of these programs and then import it into Paint Shop Pro 4.0. After your graphic is in Paint Shop Pro 4.0, you can add some special effects or do some fine tuning before saving it in the web-ready format of your choice.

Web-Specific File Types

For the time being, you have two main options to choose between for your web graphics—GIF and JPG, the file formats most graphical browsers can read. In addition, with the advent of plug-ins, more and more browsers are able to read PNG files as well.

Each of these three formats has its strengths and weaknesses, like anything else. As I get further along, I'll take a look at the two most popular formats, GIF and JPG, as well as the PNG format, and examine the reasons for using one format over another and when you'd do so.

GIF

GIF stands for Graphical Interchange Format and was developed to enable CompuServe members to exchange graphical files. A nice feature of the latest specification, GIF89a, is the capability to choose a color that will not display (be transparent) when placed over another image. This is useful if you want your image to appear in a shape other than square or rectangular. GIF89a is also used heavily on the web when a page has a background pattern the designer wants to be visible through parts of the graphic. When saving a GIF file with Paint Shop Pro 4.0, you can specify which color, if any, you want to be transparent. Likewise, you can preview how the image will appear with the transparent color in effect (this will be discussed later in the chapter in the section on Transparent GIFs).

One drawback of GIF files is the limited color palette—GIFs can have only 256 colors. This isn't all that bad, though, because many users still surf on machines that are only capable of displaying 256 colors. When you are designing your graphic, however, even if you plan on saving the final image as a GIF, you should start out with the color resolution set to 16.7 million colors. Without this color resolution, many of Paint Shop Pro's features won't be available to you. Only when you have finished designing your graphic should you set or reset the color depth to 256 colors by selecting Colors,

Decrease Color Depth. In any event, you should also save a full-color version of your graphic in a 24-bit format such as BMP. This way, if you ever want to edit or change the image, you won't have to start over from scratch.

GIF advantages	GIF disadvantages
No color information lost	Can only compress images of 256 colors (8 bits) or less
Can use different color depths below 256 colors	Doesn't compress photographs well
Compresses line art well	Copyrighted format such that developers must pay a royalty
Format read by all graphical browsers	
Image can have a transparent portion	
Fairly quick de-compression times	
Interlaced images possible	
Animation possible	

JPG

JPG (actually JPEG) stands for Joint Photographic Experts Group. This compression format is known as *lossy*, meaning when the image is compressed, some of the information is discarded or "lost." But this isn't as bad as it sounds. This compression algorithm is based on how the human eye perceives colors. A good JPG compression variant will give quite good compression and leave the image virtually unchanged, at least as far as the human eye can tell.

Unfortunately, JPG has a bad rap on the Internet, due for the most part to the dithering that takes place on systems not capable of displaying more than 256 colors. On these systems, a good GIF file will probably look a lot better than a poorly dithered JPG. On systems capable of 16-bit or 24-bit color, a JPG image will (if compressed with a high-quality setting) far surpass the quality of a GIF image. In some cases the JPG setting will even result in a much smaller file. Due to the lossy compression algorithm of the JPG format, it is especially important to save a 24-bit copy of any image you create and later save as a JPG. This is true because the lossy compression will degrade your image more and more as you save, load, edit, and re-save, eventually resulting in a very poor-quality image. Just remember to save a copy of your noncompressed image in BMP and you'll be all right. For more information on the JPG file format, you can read the JPG FAQ (Frequently Asked Questions), published regularly on the major graphics newsgroups, such as comp.graphics.misc.

JPG advantages	JPG disadvantages	PNG advantages	PNG disadvantages
Compresses photographs well	Loses some image information	No color information lost	Not yet implemented by top browsers
Possible to select compression ratio versus quality	Degradation of image possible with repeated editing and saving	Can use all color depths	
Format (now) read by all graphical browsers	No transparent portions of image are possible	Compresses well	
Progressive (interlaced) images possible	Fairly long de-compression times	Image can have a transparent portion	
Copyright allows for free use of source code to developers	Images can dither badly on 8-bit displays	Copyright allows for free use of source code by developers	
	No animation		

PNG

PNG, Portable Network Graphics, (pronounced "ping") is a relatively new compression algorithm that came into being as a result of the recent copyright issues surrounding the GIF format. PNG, a format being developed by programmers from around the world who frequent the Internet, supports some of the best qualities of both GIF and JPG, such as high compression ratios, 24-bit color, and transparent background color. PNG is quickly becoming a popular alternative to both GIF and JPG. The next generation of graphical web browsers will most likely support this format. More information about the PNG format can be found at `http://quest.jpl.nasa.gov/PNG/`.

Converting and Manipulating Graphics Files

There will be times, as described previously, when you need to convert files from one type to another. This is frequently the case when you download graphic files from the Internet and then discover they're not in either the GIF or JPG format needed for them to be displayed on your web page. At other times, you might find yourself needing to convert many of the images you've created and saved in a 24-bit format. Paint Shop Pro shines at file conversion, and will even handle multiple conversions. This is called *batch mode conversion*. It's relatively easy to do, although there are a few "gotchas" to watch out for.

Batch Conversion

To convert several images from one format to another, select File, Batch Conversions to bring up the Batch Conversion dialog box (see fig. 3.1).

Figure 3.1

Batch Conversion
dialog box.

From here you can select all the files you need to convert. The "gotcha" I referred to happens if you're trying to convert a number of files into the GIF format. If the files you're converting have different background colors and you've decided to use a transparent background color, you'll get some rather unexpected results—in fact, the transparency feature will not work. My suggestion is not to use this method to convert files to GIF unless they all have the same background color or the background color doesn't need to be set to transparent. Even if the files you're converting to GIF have the same background color, be sure it is the same as the current background color shown in the foreground/background color swatch. If you follow these simple suggestions, the batch conversion process can be a real timesaver.

Resizing and Resampling

Resizing is an easy enough term to understand, but what exactly is resampling and why is this option sometimes grayed out in the Image menu? *Resampling* is a form of resizing, the difference being that while it changes the size of an image, resampling also does what is known as *interpolation*. As Paint Shop Pro resizes an image by using the resampling function, it attempts to figure out what color the pixels should be in the areas where pixels must be added, removed, or changed. During this process, the program must have access to all 16.7 million colors; thus, if you're working on an image with a lower color depth, the resample option will not be available.

Note

Due to its use of interpolation, the resampling method is preferred to the resizing method. Although both resizing and resampling change the size of an image, a resampled image will be of a much higher quality.

You might be wondering why any of this matters. Well, it all comes down, once again, to getting rid of the dreaded jaggies. I'll show you a couple of similar graphics and, at the same time, illustrate why the resampling option can be so important.

The oval in figure 3.2 was created at 200×100 pixels and left unchanged.

Figure 3.2

Original 200×100 oval.

It doesn't look too bad, but that's partly because of the relatively low contrast between the light blue oval and the white background, as was explained in the previous chapter on color. Let's take a look at the next graphic. Figure 3.3 was created at 400×200 and resized to 200×100.

Figure 3.3

A 400×200 oval resized to 200×100.

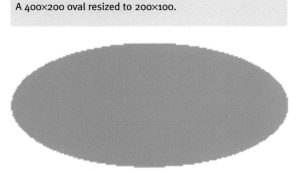

It looks pretty similar to the previous one, right? Well, what if you created the graphic at 400×200 in 16.7 million colors, and were then able to resample it instead of resizing it? The magic of mathematics would help you get a much better result. Figure 3.4 shows what the graphic looks like now.

Figure 3.4

A 400×200 oval resampled to 200×100.

Much better! This one is really smooth compared to the others. Now you can see how choosing the right colors and modes and putting options such as resampling to work can help designers achieve a polished, professional look for their graphics.

Cropping and Enlarging

Are there any other reasons you might want to crop or enlarge an image? You bet there are! What if you scan in a photo to use on your web page and later find it takes an unacceptably long time to load? Or what if you decide you don't need the whole photo, but only a part of it? (Uncle Bob wasn't really in that wedding photo, was he?) Or what about all that white space around the spiffy text graphic you want to use as a logo?

This is where cropping comes in. Sometimes, because of the way data compression works, and because of the way an image grows in file size compared to its visual size, you can save a lot of space and download time by cropping the graphic.

An uncompressed 256-color (8-bit) graphic takes up its width times its height in memory (times its color resolution in bytes—in this case, 1). For example, a 400×400 pixel image takes up 160,000 bytes and a 200×200 pixel graphic takes up only 40,000 bytes.

The smaller graphic is not half the size of the larger one—it is one quarter the size of the larger one. What all this means is if you're

careful about including only graphical information that is actually needed, you'll get much better load times for your readers. Result: Readers might actually stick around long enough to see what your site has to offer, rather than leaving after waiting two or three minutes for your large images to load.

Although this section is titled "Cropping and Enlarging," I'm not going to say much about enlarging except *don't*! I say this because current software technology does not allow for doing so without loss of image quality. The examples you see on TV and in the movies of image enhancement with enlarging just aren't possible; what you see there is actually movie magic. When you enlarge an image, the program you're using must fill in the empty pixels as it increases the dimensions of the image. This is done by using mathematics, and although the available software is fairly sophisticated, it can't really do a great job of creating the missing information. As an example, figure 3.5 shows part of a photo portrait I scanned in.

Figure 3.5

Portion of scanned photo.

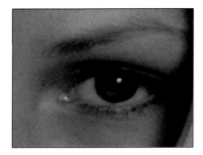

The scanned photo is quite sharp. Now look at it enlarged to twice its height and width by resampling (see fig. 3.6).

You can start to see the *pixelation*, and you might notice that the photo is losing some of its sharpness. After enlarging the image once more, the inherent problems will become more obvious. I used resampling to double both the height and width once more (see fig. 3.7). At this resolution the pixelation is very obvious. On a photograph not as sharp as this one, the details would start to disappear as well.

Figure 3.6

Portion of scanned photo enlarged two times.

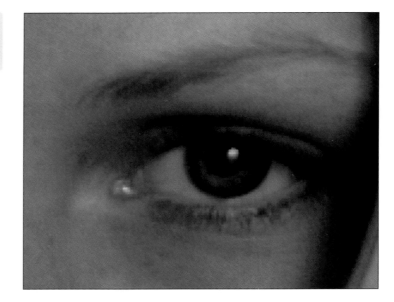

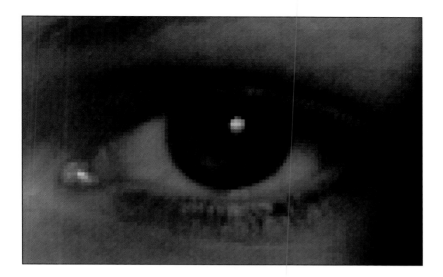

There's another reason not to enlarge your graphics unnecessarily: by doing so, you increase the file size and, thereby, the download time. Although I cropped the photos in the above examples, the first enlargement is four times the size of the original. If the second enlargement had not been cropped, it would be a whopping 16 times bigger than the original.

All of this doesn't mean you shouldn't try to create different effects by enlarging your graphics. It just means you should be prepared to lose some detail and gain some file size if you choose to enlarge.

Antialiasing

"Jaggies" are often discussed in the web graphics newsgroups on the Internet (see "Resources on the Internet" in the Appendix for information on newsgroups). For the most part, people want to know how to prevent or get rid of jaggies, and they are usually discussing the jaggies in relation to the text on their graphics. Figures 3.8 and 3.9 illustrate *jaggies*.

Help for combating the jaggies arrives in the form of *antialiasing*. In higher-end programs you can use antialiasing to smooth out images and parts of images. In Paint Shop Pro, this option is available for text. Whenever you activate the Text tool, a dialog box opens that enables you to enter text. There are several options available in this dialog box, one of which is Antialias.

What does this option do, and how does it do it? To help you understand the answers to these questions, take a look at a sample of aliased text (see fig. 3.8).

Figure 3.8

Aliased text.

Alias

Figure 3.9

Antialiased text.

Anti-Alias

Pretty jagged-looking, right? Now, look at the same text, using the same font and size but with antialiasing turned on (see fig. 3.9).

Much better! Compare the capital **A** in both images. You'll notice that the antialiased text is much less jagged than the aliased one. What did Paint Shop Pro do? Take a closer look at the text and see. In figure 3.10, you'll see the aliased text at 6:1 zoom.

At this resolution, the pixels that make up the letter are very square. Because you can't actually change that, what can be done to smooth out the letters? The answer is simple, yet on another level quite complex. How our eyes perceive objects, colors, and patterns is the complex part of the answer. Fortunately, you don't have to get into a discussion of physiology here, all you need to know is that the eye can be easily fooled. If you add some pixels whose color is between that of the letters and the background, your eye will believe the jaggedness—that's actually still there—is gone. Now take a look at the antialiased letter at the same 6:1 resolution (see fig. 3.11).

Figure 3.10

Aliased text enlarged six times.

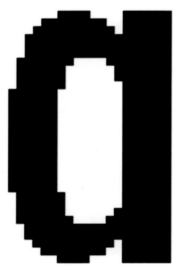

Figure 3.11

Antialiased text enlarged six times.

See those pixels that are made up of various shades of gray? The program puts them there when you select the Antialias option. Of course, at this resolution you can see the extra pixels, but when you look at the text at the size you created it, all you see is nice, smooth text. A kind of magic, eh? Okay, not really, but remember why you do this and it'll help you get rid of the jaggies on your lettering.

This solution seems simple enough, but there is a problem. Sometimes when you select the Text tool, you find the Antialias option grayed out (in versions prior to 4.0 it is grayed out; in 4.0 and above, the option might be available but have no effect). Again, the reason for this is complex, but the solution is simple. When Paint Shop Pro performs the mathematics involved in calculating and applying those in-between colors, it needs to be able to choose from as many colors as possible. If the graphic you're working on has a color depth of less than 16.7 million colors, Paint Shop Pro 3.xx won't allow you to choose the Antialias option. Paint Shop Pro 4.0 will let you choose it but not apply it. The way around this is to always start with 16.7 million colors. After you finish the image, you can, if necessary, decrease the color resolution. But what if you are working on a 256-color GIF image, for example, and you want to add antialiased text? Simple! Increase the color resolution by choosing Colors, Increase Color Depth, 16.7 Million Colors. Add the text and then decrease the resolution by choosing Colors, Decrease Color Depth, 256 Colors before resaving the GIF. This will give your finished product a more professional appearance.

Even though antialiasing only appears as an option with the Text tool, it is available when using the drawing tools at 16.7 million colors. Figure 3.12 shows a line drawn with the brush tool, in which the graphic's color depth is set at 16.7 million colors.

Figure 3.12

Antialiased line.

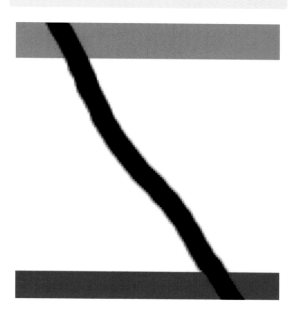

Notice the antialiasing. It is present in the pixels whose color lies between the color of the line and the colors the line goes through. In other words, where the line goes through the white, you can see some shades of gray between the line and the white background.

Figure 3.13 shows the same kind of line drawn with the brush tool, but at 256 colors.

Figure 3.13

Aliased line.

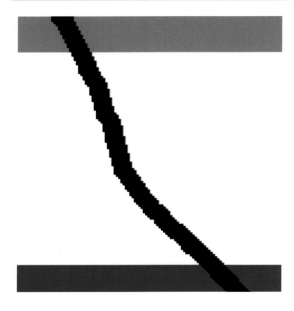

Of course, you're just viewing these examples on the pages of a book. To get the full effect I recommend that you take a minute to draw a couple of these ovals with Paint Shop Pro, using the discussed methods, and see how dramatic the difference really is.

should be, you'll have to play around with the image you're creating, because this technique is somewhat dependent on the size of the image. I'll examine, once again, some examples of 200×100 ovals.

Figure 3.14 was drawn with the Shape tool. It's pretty jagged, just as you would expect from what you've learned so far.

You'll see that this example is very jagged compared to the previous one.

These are a couple more very good reasons to always start, and save, your images in 16.7 million colors, as the following topics show.

Feathering

Feathering is another option new to Paint Shop Pro 4.0 that can help kill jagged edges. You can use this technique when drawing certain shapes. Instead of using the Shape tool to create an oval, for example, you can use the Selection tool with the Feathering option set to an appropriate value. To figure out what that value

Figure 3.14

Oval drawn with Shape tool.

Figure 3.15 was drawn by using the Selection tool, with the Feathering option set to 2 and the selection type set to Ellipse. The selection was then filled by using the Fill tool. It's a little smoother, but not yet acceptable.

Figure 3.15

Oval created with Selection tool and filled with Fill tool.

Figure 3.16 was created the same way, but the feathering was set to 10. It is even smoother. The edges are starting to get a little too soft, though. The best result, seen in figure 3.17, was created by using a combination of a couple of the methods you've already seen.

Figure 3.16

Oval created as in figure 3.15, but with Feather set to 10.

Figure 3.17 was created at 400×200, using the Selection tool with Feathering set at 10. It was then resampled down to 200×100. Given that this oval was created by using the same program as the preceding ones and that it will be displayed on the same system as the others, it certainly looks much more professional. It's not jagged and its edges are not too soft. (This

can't be done by the numbers. As usual, you should play around with the program and its options to find what gives you the best result.)

Figure 3.17

Oval created as in figure 3.15, but at 400×200 and then resampled to 200×100.

GIF or JPG?

Although the web is a fast-moving and ever-changing entity, you are currently limited to only two choices for your graphics file-types: GIF and JPG. Both of these utilize compression algorithms, which is a fancy way of saying they take the electronic information that makes up a digital graphic and, through the use of a mathematical formula, make that large amount of information smaller. The difference is that the formulas compress the data in different ways. You don't necessarily need to know the differences in the math, but rather how those differences influence the choice of which format you'll use for a particular graphic.

Some people find the differences a little confusing and therefore stick to using GIF. This can be a mistake, however, and something of a disadvantage. Naturally, there are times when GIF is the appropriate choice. For example, if your graphic needs a transparent background, your only choice would be GIF. JPG does not have this capability due to its *lossy* compression method. There are other reasons you would want to choose one format over the other, but the rules when making a choice are not hard and fast.

So, when should you choose one format over the other? It really depends on the graphic. If the graphic is a simple black-and-white line drawing, or a picture with (relatively) large areas of equal color, GIF is the way to go. On the other hand, if you have a picture that is best described as "photo-like," you should go with JPG. In the first case you'll get a much smaller file, and in the second case a JPG will likely be compressed to a smaller size, thereby reducing the loading time for your readers. You wouldn't want to use the JPG format, though, if you have a picture with large areas of the same color. If you do use JPG in this case, not only will you not get a better compression rate, but you will end up with *artifacts*. To see what this is like, look at the JPG-formatted graphic shown in figure 3.18. (If you want to read more about the use of GIF format versus JPG, see "Resources on the Internet" in the Appendix.)

Figure 3.18

Oval before saving as JPG.

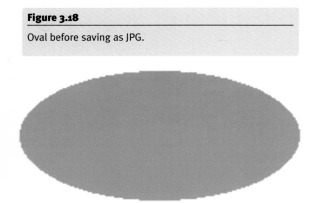

Because of the way the JPG compression algorithm works, and because this ellipse is a solid color, the result of saving this graphic as a JPG results in the image seen in figure 3.19.

Figure 3.19

Oval with artifacts created by saving as JPG.

The dark halo around the edge of the ellipse is composed of *artifacts*. You see, the original information has actually been changed! The way a JPG compresses a file is by discarding some of the information—this is why it's called a *lossy* compression technique. This is, of course, a problem if you're compressing something like the preceding graphic. If, on the other hand, you're working with a photo, the information that's lost won't be readily evident to the human eye and can, in fact, result in a much smaller yet better quality image than GIF. Why is the result of better quality? Because the JPG format will store a file with 24 bits of information, using up to 16.7 million colors, and a GIF file will use only 8 bits, or 256 colors.

Figure 3.20 shows a portrait that was scanned in full 24-bit mode. It's 394×380 pixels, contains 44,537 colors, and has a file size of 449,974 bytes.

Figure 3.20

Marianne scanned at 24 bits.

The next version (see fig. 3.21) of the same scan has been saved as a JPG. It still has the same dimensions but now contains 23,979 colors. You'd be hard pressed to see which colors are missing and even to see much difference between the two photos. The JPG, though, only occupies 23,122 bytes! That's a large saving over the original scan.

In figure 3.22 the photo was saved as a GIF. It still has the same dimensions as the other two; however, the difference in quality is pretty obvious. There are only 250 colors used in this graphic. Although its quality might be acceptable for web use, this 250-color GIF occupies a whopping 119,138 bytes instead of the 23,122 bytes (and 23,979 colors) in the JPG version.

Figure 3.21

Marianne scan saved as a 24-bit JPG.

Figure 3.22

Marianne scan saved as an 8-bit GIF.

It's obvious then that, under these conditions, JPG would be the best option to use, even with its lossy compression format.

Lossy Versus Lossless Compression

The lossy part of the JPG format can cause something of a problem. Let's say you start out with a 24-bit scanned photo. You convert it to JPG, not only to save room but also to use your image on the web. Great! No problem— yet. But let's say in the future you need to make some changes to that photo. Maybe you want to reduce its size because it's still a little large and your readers have commented on how long it takes to load. You can just take that JPG file and resample or resize it to decrease the dimensions. But if you do, you're taking a graphic that has already "lost" some information; reducing it, which loses more information; and then re-saving it as a JPG, further degrading the graphic.

To see what can happen if you choose to edit and resave a JPG file, take a look at the next two graphics. Figure 3.23 was created and saved as a JPG. Because it has only three colors, it's not a good candidate for JPG to begin with, and you can see the artifacts around the letters.

After opening and saving this file five times, there has been a marked deterioration, especially around the last letter in each word (see fig. 3.24).

■**Definition**▬▬▬▬▬▬▬▬▬▬

Lossy refers to the compression method used by the JPG file format. When compressing an image, the JPG format actually discards or loses some of the information in a graphic image. Although some of the information is lost, this format can result in huge savings in file size. When this technique is used on photographic-type images, the missing information is not readily apparent to the human eye.

Figure 3.23

Graphic showing some artifacts after saving as JPG.

Figure 3.24

Graphic showing further deterioration after opening and saving as JPG five times.

What can be done in this situation? The answer is simple. Keep a copy of the scan in its original 24-bit format, whether that's BMP or some other lossless format. Then, when you find you need to change the graphic, start with the original again. In the case of the example graphic here, you could reload the scan and resample or edit it, then save it again to the JPG format, and upload it to replace the larger image. This way the lossy compression is only done once on the image, you end up with a good quality image that's a little smaller or edited in some other way, and your readers still get faster load times and higher-quality graphics when viewing your web page.

Compression and Color Depth

The number of colors in a graphic can also be a factor when you are deciding which format to use. For example, it would not be an ideal choice to save a line drawing with only two colors, black and white, as a JPG. Not only will you get a smaller file with no artifacts if you save it as a GIF, but you only need a couple of colors in the first place. In fact, if you load, change, and re-save a black-and-white graphic as a JPG, the file size might actually get larger every time you do, and the quality will deteriorate, as in the earlier examples.

The color depth (number of colors) in an image can actually be a factor in the compressed size of the resulting file. A file with only two colors, such as a line drawing, will actually be larger when saved as a 256-color GIF than the same file saved as a 2-color GIF. The image of Billy diNerdo (a character from an online comic strip I created) shown in figure 3.25 is 1,938 bytes when saved as a 256-color GIF, yet it's only 1,066 bytes when saved as a 2-color GIF—and with no loss in quality. The same image saved as a 256-shade grayscale JPG is a whopping 6,427 bytes!

Figure 3.25

Billy diNerdo line drawing.

If Billy were colored in—instead of just black-and-white—other choices would have to be made. It might happen, though, that 16 colors would be enough for this online comic, and file size and load time could still remain smaller and quicker if Billy were saved as a 16-color GIF.

Transparent GIFs

There is one instance when the choice of which graphic format to use is clear. When you need to set a certain color as transparent, the only choice (for now, anyway) is GIF. When you want to create a text logo and display it against a web page that contains a textured background, you'll need to use the GIF format. Or, say you have a graphic with a distinctive irregular shape you'd like to preserve; this can also only be done by saving the image as a GIF.

■ Note

See the tutorial on creating Transparent GIFs in Chapter 8, "Special Techniques."

Interlaced GIFs and Progressive JPGs

One property GIFs and JPGs share, as well as PNGs for that matter, is interlacing, referred to as *progression* when JPGs are being discussed. *Interlacing* describes the capability of the software, in this case the web browser, to display the image a little at a time. Rather than the whole image being drawn from top to bottom in sequence, the lines are displayed in steps. To get an idea of how this works, imagine the software displaying only the odd-numbered lines (1, 3, 5, 7...) of the image first. Then, after all the odd-numbered lines have been drawn, the software displays all the even-numbered lines (2, 4, 6, 8...).

Saving your images with one of these methods (interlaced for GIFs and progressive for JPGs) gives viewers of your pages a chance to see what the image will be before it has been completely downloaded. One drawback to using this method for displaying your images becomes obvious when the images contain textual information. If the viewer decides to interrupt the transfer of the image, there is a chance the text will be totally unreadable.

Most browsers and most image-processing programs—Paint Shop Pro included—support both interlaced GIFs and progressive JPGs. Whether to use this format when you save your files is something you'll have to decide for yourself; personally, I prefer to keep my images

In actuality, there is a larger gap between the lines being displayed and those yet to be drawn, causing the image to have a grainy appearance at first and then gradually become more clear as the missing lines fill in. If you view an interlaced graphic from your system's hard drive, the progression from a grainy image to the final image can take place fairly quickly. When the image's information is being downloaded from your web site to a reader's system, on the other hand, this process can be rather lengthy, taking as long as several minutes.

small enough that load time is minimal. I do this by keeping the height and width of the images fairly small and, when possible, by reducing the color depth.

Summary: Making an Educated Guess

The choice between GIF and JPG is not always as obvious as it was in the previous examples. What should you do if you have an image that doesn't need a transparent background, isn't a line drawing, and might not be exactly photo quality?

In this case, I recommend saving the graphic as both file types, GIF and JPG, and then checking to see which format gives the smallest compressed file size and/or the best-quality image. The result of such a comparison can be surprising. In any event, when the choice can go either way, stick with the one that gives you a combination of the smallest file size and the best image quality. Sometimes you have to choose between image quality and size, when the smaller image leaves you with less than acceptable quality or the better-quality image is prohibitively large.

Because the image will be going on your web site, you'll have to make the final choice yourself, unless, of course, someone is paying you to design their graphics. Armed with knowledge from this section, though, you will at least be able to make or offer an informed decision.

Chapter 4

Essential Elements of Your Web Page

This chapter covers the essential parts of a web page. I doubt you can find many web pages these days that don't have at least some buttons, bars, or custom bullets. Although I won't be able to show you how to create every type of button, bar, or bullet you can imagine, I hope to give you several ideas you can build on.

Topics covered in this section.

▶ Bullets

▶ Balls

▶ Bars

▶ Buttons

    ▶ Rectangular Buttons

    ▶ Beveled Rectangular Buttons

    ▶ Round Buttons

    ▶ Oval Buttons

▶ Icons

▶ 3D Buttons

In the following sections of the book, I'm going to spend some time explaining the "how's and why's" of the images I've created with Paint Shop Pro. It is my hope that after reading the tutorials and trying out the techniques, you will explore even more of this wonderful program on your own. By using the formulas I have set down in these pages, you will be able to design and create some unique-looking images for your web site; but I'd like to think that along the way I've helped inspire you to do more than that—that you will play around and let your imagination take over. I'm constantly amazed by the many people who, after exploring my web site and going through some of my on-line tutorials, e-mail me and send me a graphic they've created. These terrific folks have taken my examples to new heights, doing things I'd never imagined. To me, this is part of the artistic process, each of us building on what others have done.

Most of all, I'd like you to have fun; if you enjoy designing and creating your web pages, people will have fun when they surf by to check them out.

This first section covers what I call the essential elements of your page, because you really can't have a web page without having some sort of bullets, bars, or buttons. More than mere decoration, these elements help organize your pages. *Bullets* are useful for organizing and presenting lists, *bars* help to visually separate different parts of a page, and *buttons* provide a method of navigation to help visitors explore your site.

Designing Your Own Bullets

HTML implements two forms of lists, one of which uses built-in bullets to visually organize a collection of information. Using this built-in function is relatively easy, of course, but it can also be rather dull.

A better alternative is to design your own bullets. All you need is a small graphic to place at

the beginning of each list item. This graphic can be almost any shape you can imagine. You can also use shadows or colorful highlights to help make the bullets more visually appealing. Figure 4.1 takes a look at some examples.

Figure 4.1

Sample bullets.

The buttons shown in figure 4.1 were created by using either the Shape tool or the Selection tool to create the shapes and then applying drop shadows. After these shapes have been resampled down to a smaller size, 20×20 or so, they can be used as bullets for lists. You can use practically any shape for this purpose—as long as it's small. You can color your bullets to suit the mood of your page. You might even get creative and shrink down parts of photos.

■Note

My web site, in its current incarnation, can be seen at http://www.grafx-design.com. It contains some online tutorials for Paint Shop Pro and Photoshop, as well as links to my web design business, *Earth Orbit*, and my digital art work. I hope to have some of the textures and other graphics from this book available online by the time you read the book.

You can reach me via e-mail at tmc@grafx-design.com. I don't promise to reply to everyone—I really can't, considering the amount of e-mail I receive—but I definitely read each and every one.

Essential Elements of Your Web Page

Tip

You should be aware that, even though a bullet graphic is stored once and used repeatedly, it takes time to download. Keeping this in mind, try to size your bullets accordingly. A 20×20 graphic is quite small, while a 50×50 is substantially bigger, at least as far as decorative graphics go.

The white examples can be saved with white as the transparent color and then used on a page that has a textured background; however, you must make sure the shadow stands out enough. If necessary, you can set the vertical and horizontal offset higher in the Drop Shadow dialog box to increase the size of the shadow and, thereby, the visibility of the bullet. Figure 4.2 shows an example of this style of button against the paper background from the tutorial pages of the GrafX site.

Figure 4.2

Sample bullets against a textured background.

PSP Tutorials
3D Buttons
Bevelled Text
Drop Shadows
Seamless Tiles

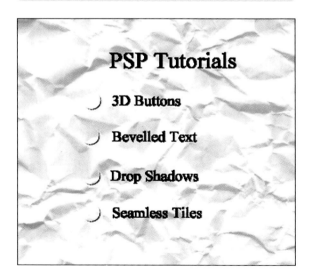

The bullets in this example are quite subtle. In another case something more flamboyant might be called for. Part of the fun in designing your pages is making the decisions about the look you want to achieve. Since web pages can and should be changed and updated fairly frequently, you don't have to be stuck with any certain look.

HTML editors also offer numbered lists as an option, and so does Paint Shop Pro. Using Paint Shop Pro, you can use any font you have on your system to come up with a look that will mesh well with the "flavor" of your pages (see fig. 4.3).

Figure 4.3

Sample numbered list, using graphic fonts.

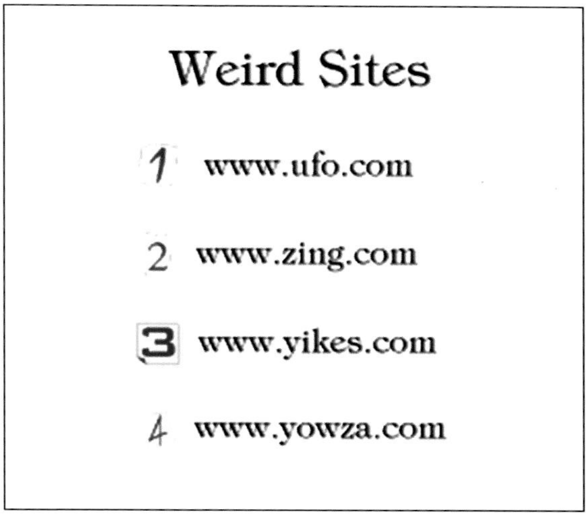

Weird Sites
1 www.ufo.com
2 www.zing.com
3 www.yikes.com
4 www.yowza.com

You're not even limited to the system fonts. If you wanted to, you could simply draw the numbers and use the resulting images as the numbered bullets for your lists. Take a look at some of the text techniques in Chapter 5, "Getting Your Message Across," for ideas you can use.

Creating 3D Balls: Another Alternative to Boring Bullets

Rather than use the boring bullets supplied by web browsers, some web masters like to highlight their online documents with 3D balls. Here's a look at one method for creating them.

Start with a 100×100 graphic, making sure you open the file in 16.7 million colors. If you plan on placing the balls against a textured background, choose a background color for your graphic that closely matches the predominant color of your texture. In this example, I'll be using white.

First, select a medium gray foreground color and draw a Filled Oval shape near the bottom of the graphic using the Shapes tool (see fig. 4.4).

Select Image, Normal Filters, Blur More and blur the oval a couple of times until it resembles figure 4.5. This will be the shadow of your ball.

Figure 4.4

Oval shape for shadow.

Figure 4.5

Shadow oval blurred.

Select the foreground color you want for the ball. Draw it in with the Shapes tool as above, but this time make the shape round. Offset the ball a little to the left and overlap it into the shadow as shown in figure 4.6.

Figure 4.6

Round shape placed over shadow.

Click the foreground color swatch to bring up the Color dialog box. Now, because you are using 16.7 million colors (24-bit), you can keep the same basic color but select a different shade. There's a slider along the right side of the Color dialog box. Move the slider down to get a darker shade of your color.

Select the Airbrush tool with a setting of 10, 50.

Tip

If you think you might be a little unsteady, you can use the Magic Wand tool to select the ball. With the ball selected, the Airbrush tool will paint only inside the selection.

Using the Airbrush tool, draw a crescent shape within the lower right part of the circle to create a shadow on the sphere. If you don't like the results, select Edit, Undo and try again. Your graphic should resemble figure 4.7.

Figure 4.7

Shadow added to ball.

Click the foreground color swatch again and this time, in the Color dialog box, move the slider up to get a lighter shade of your chosen color.

Change the size setting of the Airbrush to 6 or 7, making it a little smaller, and spray a small circular shape in the upper left corner of the circle to form part of the highlight on the sphere (see fig. 4.8).

Now set the foreground color to white and shrink the Airbrush size down to 2 or 3. Spray a small dot of white in the lighter circle created in the last step (see fig. 4.9).

Great! Now shrink the ball down to bullet size and save it as a web-ready GIF. I shrank the ball shown in figure 4.10 down to 30×30. You can even go a little smaller, depending on the text you'll be placing it next to. Remember, too, the smaller the image, the smaller the final file size.

Figure 4.8

Highlight added to ball.

Figure 4.9

Additional highlight added to ball.

Figure 4.10

Final web-ready ball.

You can make balls like these out of any color you prefer. The Fill tool can also be used to create balls. First, create a shadow graphic again (see fig. 4.11), using the same steps that led to figure 4.5.

Figure 4.11

Blurred oval shadow.

Choose the Selection tool and set the Selection Type to Circle. Draw a circular selection and fill it in by using the Fill tool (see fig. 4.12).

The settings I used were:

▶ Sunburst Gradient

▶ 73% Vertical

▶ 16% Horizontal

I used R:177 G:243 B:243 for the light blue and R:1 G:3 B:215 for the dark blue. Because the selection for the ball partly covered the

shadow, I set the tolerance to 120 so the fill would work over both the white area and the dark gray of the shadow. I had tried a lower setting for the tolerance, but the shadow wasn't being filled in. You can see that sometimes you must play around with the settings of the various options to achieve the desired look.

Figure 4.12

Ball created by using gradient fill.

Note

The Tolerance option is a useful option to learn more about. I suggest you play with the settings on a couple of images to get a feel for this. Tolerance can be set on the Magic Wand, the Fill tool, and the Color Replacer. Changing the values will drastically change how a tool's effects are applied.

With the Fill tool, however, another option is to use the Match Mode. For example, try setting the Match Mode to None in the previous step as an alternative to playing with the Tolerance setting.

This method is somewhat easier than the first was, but what you learned by designing the first ball will come in handy when you wish to create textured balls.

If you're daring enough, you can give this next technique a try. Find a textured graphic. Use the Selection tool, with the Selection Type set to circle, to cut a circle out of the textured graphic. Then paste the circle over the shadow. Use the same steps as those above, in the first example, to shade and highlight the circle, but choose a color that's already in the texture. Darkening and lightening this color will produce the desired result, similar to that shown in figure 4.13.

For an even better effect, try this. Create an oval shadow. Then, take a textured graphic like the one shown in figure 4.14 and use the Selection tool to cut a square shape from it. I cut a 70×70 pixel portion from the textured graphic.

Select Image, Deformations, Circle to deform the square into a sphere (see fig. 4.15).

Tip

Play around with the settings of the Airbrush. Open a second graphic as a scratch pad to try out the different colors and settings—opacity, size, and flow—before applying them to the original.

Figure 4.13

Textured ball.

Figure 4.14

70×70 pixel image cropped from textured graphic.

Figure 4.15

Image transformed into sphere.

Now choose Selections, Select, All and copy the whole graphic, and then Edit, Paste, As Transparent Selection to paste the textured sphere over the shadow, as in figure 4.16.

Figure 4.16

Sphere pasted over oval shadow.

You'll probably notice that the antialiasing has left a line of white at the bottom of the ball where it meets the shadow. Next I'll tell you how to use the Retouch tool to get rid of that line (see fig. 4.17).

Figure 4.17

Retouch tool.

After selecting the Retouch tool, set the options as follows:

▶ Retouch Mode: Soften

▶ Size: 2

▶ Shape: Round

▶ Opacity: 75

▶ Paper Texture: None

Drag the mouse around the area where the line is, smoothing the difference between the colors created by the antialiasing. With practice, this will become easier. The result should be similar to that shown in figure 4.18.

Figure 4.18

Touched-up area between sphere and shadow.

You still need to add highlights and shadows to complete the effect. There are several ways to accomplish this, one of which would be to use the Retouch tool set at Lighten/Darken.

Another method involves using the Lasso Selection tool (see fig. 4.19).

Figure 4.19

Lasso selection tool.

Select the Lasso selection tool with the Feather option set to 3 or 4 and draw a crescent moon shape in the bottom right part of the sphere. You might want to zoom-in for this as I did in figure 4.20.

Figure 4.20

Area of sphere selected for shadow.

■ Note

The Feathering value changes how hard or soft the selected area will be. A higher value makes the edges of the selection softer, while a lower value makes the edges harder.

Choose Colors, Adjust, Brightness/Contrast, with contrast set to 0 and brightness set to −10 to add a shadow, and your graphic will now resemble figure 4.21.

Figure 4.21

Shadow added to sphere.

De-select the current selection by choosing Selections, None from the menu.

Use the Lasso tool again to draw a circular shape in the upper left of the sphere (see fig. 4.22).

Choose Colors, Adjust, Brightness/Contrast again, but this time use a positive value to get a highlight. I used 10 and left the contrast at 0. I found this wasn't bright enough for the effect I wanted, so I used Edit, Undo and then tried a brightness setting of 15. It still wasn't bright enough. I used Edit, Undo once more and tried a brightness setting of 20. This value produced the effect I was looking for (see fig. 4.23).

I then dragged the mouse around the middle of the highlighted area until I achieved the final effect (see fig. 4.24).

Figure 4.22

Area of sphere selected for highlight.

Figure 4.23

Highlight added to sphere.

Figure 4.24

Final textured sphere.

To add the final touch—a bright spot within the highlighted area—I selected the Retouch tool and used the following settings:

- ▶ h Mode: Lighten
- ▶ Size: 2
- ▶ Shape: Round
- ▶ Opacity: 15
- ▶ Paper Texture: None

After this graphic has been resampled down in size and saved as a GIF or JPG, you'll have a truly unique ball to use on your web pages.

(For help in deciding which form to save it in, you can review the discussion of GIF and JPG in Chapter 3, "Graphics Quality.")

If you can't find any textured graphics, it's fairly simple to create patterns yourself by using Paint Shop Pro. This topic will be covered in Chapter 6, "Backgrounds and Borders."

Designing Separator Bars

Separator bars are a good way to help distinguish one part of your web page from another. There are many ways of designing separator bars, depending on your taste and the content and color scheme of your site.

You can vary the shape, the color, and the size of the bars. You can use a solid color, a texture, some clip art, or just about anything. You can use shadows or not—it's all up to you. Here are a couple of ideas to get you started.

For the first one I created a new graphic of 450×30×16.7 million colors and drew a long, dark gray rectangle in it, using the Shape tool (see fig. 4.25).

Using Image, Normal Filters, Blur Mode, I blurred the rectangle a few times to soften it up and make it look more like a shadow (see fig. 4.26).

At this point I chose a foreground color and drew another rectangle over the shadow, instantly creating a basic bar (see fig. 4.27).

These are so easy to create that you should play around with different sizes and colors to see what looks best on your web pages.

A neat variation is to take a large image and, using the Rectangle Selection tool, copy and paste a section of the image over the shadow graphic, as I did in figure 4.28.

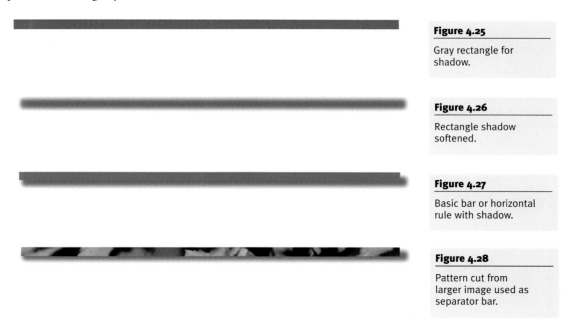

Figure 4.25

Gray rectangle for shadow.

Figure 4.26

Rectangle shadow softened.

Figure 4.27

Basic bar or horizontal rule with shadow.

Figure 4.28

Pattern cut from larger image used as separator bar.

▌Tip ▐████████████████████

If you're going to use this shadow with several different bars, you should save it separately so you don't have to re-create it every time.

▌Note ▐████████████████████

With Paint Shop Pro 4.0, of course, you can just choose Image, Special Effects, Drop Shadow to add a shadow to the bar.

This one is from a photo of fall leaves I scanned in. If I needed several bars, I could copy different parts of the photo to slightly alter the graphic each time.

Another great idea is to use clip art. Select something that goes with the scheme of your site. Create a long, rectangular graphic that has the same height as the clip art, and copy-and-paste the clip art into the graphic until it's full (see fig. 4.29). Any repeating pattern will do. If the clip art is too large, shrink down the final bar to a more manageable size after you have finished pasting the clip art in.

One variation on this idea would be to rotate the clip art as you paste it into the graphic. Some really neat patterns can be created, so I suggest you play around and see what you can come up with.

In the section on "Drawing With Selections" in Chapter 8, "Special Techniques," I'll describe how the round-ended gold bars I used on the Graf X site were created (see fig. 4.30).

Building Buttons

It's almost impossible to have a web page without some sort of button, even if it's just an e-mail button. Buttons, which can come in all shapes and sizes, help your readers navigate through your web site. This is truly one area of your web page design where you are limited only by your imagination.

Let's start with something relatively simple and progress to some wilder and more elaborate designs.

Rectangle Buttons

The most simple button to create is a plain-colored rectangle. Use the Shape tool with the following options set:

- ▶ Line:1
- ▶ Shape: Rectangle
- ▶ Style: Filled

Figure 4.29

Bar created with clip art.

Figure 4.30

Separator bar created by using special techniques and filters.

Draw a rectangle. I created a new 200×100 graphic with 16.7 million colors and the default white background (see fig. 4.31).

Add some text. I used the Uptight Neon font with size set at 26 and antialiasing turned on (see fig. 4.32).

Figure 4.31

Simple rectangle.

Figure 4.32

Text added to button.

Beveled Rectangular Buttons

A little dimension can be added by beveling the edges of the button. Start off as before with a filled rectangle (see fig. 4.33).

Click on the foreground color swatch to bring up the Color dialog box. If you're in 16.7 million color mode, as you should be, you'll see a vertical slider bar at the top right of the dialog box (see fig. 4.34).

Figure 4.33

Simple rectangle.

Figure 4.34

Color slider in Color dialog box.

You can see what the current color is, because there is a small triangle pointer next to it. You can also see that what you have to select from here are the various shades of the current color, which makes selecting a lighter or darker shade of the same color very easy. Just click somewhere above the triangle to get a lighter shade or somewhere below to get a darker shade.

You want to achieve the effect of the light coming in from an angle and defining the shape of

Figure 4.35

Light coming from upper left.

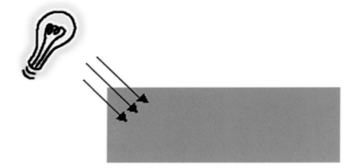

the beveled edges of the button. Imagine that the light is coming from above and to the left of the button, as in figure 4.35.

This would mean the top and left side of the button would be lighter (highlighted), while the bottom and right side would be darker (shaded). To simulate this effect, select a lighter shade of the foreground color by using the slider in the Color dialog box as described above.

Select the Line tool and draw a couple of lines along the top and left side. Thinner lines will give you a slimmer looking button, while a thicker set of lines will make the button seem fairly thick.

Draw four lines on the button, each 1 pixel wide (see fig. 4.36).

Figure 4.36

Highlight added to top and left side.

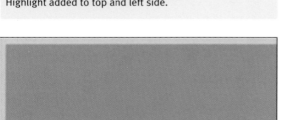

Now select a darker shade and draw the same number of lines along the bottom and the right side (see fig. 4.37).

Figure 4.37

Shadow added to bottom and right side.

The corners cannot be left like this, though, as they are squared off and don't help the illusion much. To see what I mean, zoom in and take a look at one of the corners where the highlight and shadow meet (see fig. 4.38).

To correct the squared-off look, use the shadow color and draw a diagonal line from the top right corner to the point where the shadow and highlight intersect. Repeat this procedure at the bottom left corner. Don't be afraid to zoom in so you can position the diagonal line properly. If you don't get it quite right on the first attempt, use Edit, Undo and try it again (see fig. 4.39).

Figure 4.38

Zoomed-in corner of rectangle showing squared-off highlight and shadow.

Use either the Paint tool or the Brush tool to fill in the stray light pixels (see fig. 4.41).

As a finishing touch, select a shade that's much lighter than your highlight and draw a line down from the upper left corner to where the highlight lines meet the face of the button, as in figure 4.42.

Figure 4.39

Line drawn to fix edge between highlight and shadow.

Figure 4.40

Beveled areas nearly completed.

Figure 4.41

Beveled button.

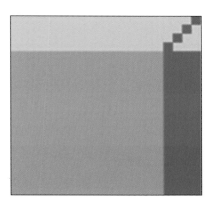

The preceding image was zoomed at 5:1. At this resolution it was fairly easy to place the diagonal lines. The graphic in figure 4.40 shows the result of these operations.

Figure 4.42

Additional highlight added.

You can see the completed beveled button in figure 4.43.

Compare the beveled button to the first button, seen again in figure 4.44.

Figure 4.43

Final beveled button.

Figure 4.44

First simple, flat, one color button.

The bevels make quite a difference. This is not to say there's anything wrong with the first button; rather, it all comes down to the look you want to achieve—simple versus more sophisticated. Because I was after an artsy look on a writers' web page I designed a while back, I used buttons like the one shown in figure 4.45.

Figure 4.45

Artsy button created for writers' web page.

To create the button in figure 4.45, all I did was select a color and set the Brush Tool to a size of 6 or so. I then drew the shape in a very loose manner, not really paying attention to the shape. When I was satisfied, I set the foreground color to white and added the text. Voilà! A 10-second artsy-looking button.

There has been a lot of chatter in the graphics newsgroups about when a button is a button and when it isn't. The preceding example might not be what you'd think of as a "classic" button, nor was it my intention to create a "button-looking" button. People have surfed the pages that use these buttons and, as far as I know, none of them have gotten lost while doing so.

I don't intend to argue about what looks like a button and what doesn't. I'd rather show you how to get as creative as you can and then let you decide what works for you and your readers. If you get a lot of e-mail from your readers because they can't navigate your site, you're either reaching the wrong audience or you should consider changing the graphics you're using. The web is a great place to try things out.

Round Buttons

Plain round buttons are just as easy to create as the plain rectangle buttons were. Achieving a beveled look on a round button, however, is more involved.

To get the beveled effect and have "3D-look" round buttons imagine, once again, that the light is coming from the top left corner of the image.

Start with a 200×200 16.7 million color image. Set the foreground color to a dark blue (I used R:41 G:5 B:165) and set the background color to a light blue (I used R:116 G:223 R:246).

Take note of the mouse coordinates at the bottom left corner of the Paint Shop Pro screen (see fig. 4.46). These two numbers, which represent the x and y coordinates of the mouse on the image, update constantly as you move the mouse over the current image.

Figure 4.46

Cursor coordinates shown in lower left corner of Paint Shop Pro screen.

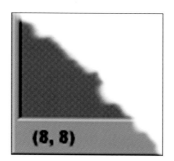

As shown in figure 4.46, we'll start at the x, y coordinates 8, 8. Use the Selection tool with Selection Type set to Circle and Feather at 4, and move the mouse to 8, 8.

Draw a circular selection that fills most of the image window, but leave enough room to add a drop shadow (see fig. 4.47).

Figure 4.47

Circular selection.

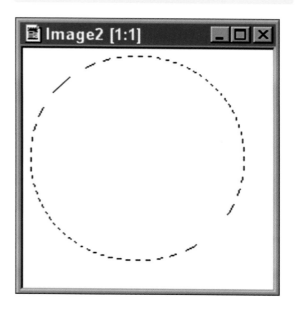

Select the Fill tool and set the Fill Style to Linear Gradient. Then click on Options and set the direction to 135 degrees.

Fill the selection, as shown in figure 4.48.

If the light were coming from the upper left, the image would appear to have a concave shape. This effect will become more apparent after the inside of the button has been completed.

Figure 4.48

Selection filled with gradient.

Figure 4.49

Second, inner selection.

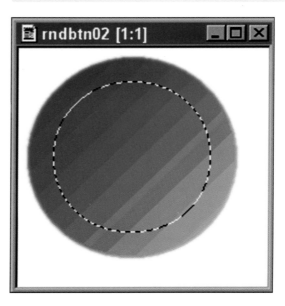

De-select the selection by choosing Selections, None.

Using the Selection tool, start at 30, 30 and draw another circle (see fig. 4.49). Try to get the inner circle to fit evenly within the outer circle.

To obtain the effect of a protruding (convex) inner circle, the direction of the gradient should be reversed, that is, the fill should go from light blue to dark blue. This can be achieved in one of two ways. You could opt to change the direction of the gradient by 180 degrees in the Linear Gradient Options dialog box, but a quicker method would be to swap the foreground and background colors. This is done by clicking on the small, bent, two-headed arrow found in the lower left corner of the foreground/background color swatch (see fig. 4.50). Clicking on the arrow toggles the two colors back and forth.

Actually a third, and easier, way exists. Right-clicking the mouse inside the selection causes the gradient fill to run in the opposite direction. Try it.

Figure 4.50

Color swatch and foreground/background swapping arrows.

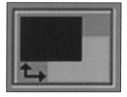

Click once on the arrow to swap the two colors. Select the Fill tool and adjust the tolerance to 50. This needs to be done because the area to be filled is not a solid color. If this number is too low, the Fill tool will fill only a part of the selected circle. Instead of playing with the

Tolerance, another option is to choose None under the Match Mode. The image should look like figure 4.51.

Figure 4.51

3D round button.

Now the curve of the inner and outer parts of this circular button are easily visible.

To apply a drop shadow, a "selection" must be made; however, the button is made up of many colors and will, therefore, be hard to select. Experimenting with various values in the Tolerance option would eventually result in a successful selection, but this method can be time-consuming, to say the least. Too low a value will select only part of the button, while too high a value will select the white background along with the button. To get around this problem, use the Magic Wand tool to select the white background, and then choose Selections, Invert. This leaves the button selected. Make sure the Feather option is set to 0 so the selection is as close as possible to the outside edge of the button.

Select Images, Special Effects, Add, Drop Shadow with the following settings, as in figure 4.52:

- ▶ Color: Black
- ▶ Opacity: 200
- ▶ Blur: 20
- ▶ Vertical Offset: 10
- ▶ Horizontal Offset: 10

Apply some text, as in figure 4.53.

Figure 4.52

Round button with drop shadow.

Figure 4.53

Text added to round button.

Or a direction arrow, as in figure 4.54.

Figure 4.54

Directional arrow added to round button.

Resample the image to the size you want. Then save it as a GIF or a JPG, and it will be ready for your web pages.

A different look can be achieved as easily as changing the direction of the gradient fill. If the fill goes from light to dark on the outside and from dark to light on the inside, the button will resemble figure 4.55.

Although the white outline caused by the anti-aliasing didn't seem too out of place on the last button because of the way the lighting was done and because of the apparent shape of the button, in figure 4.55 it causes a problem. The white outline should blend more with the shadow, because the part of the button where the line is should be in shadow. This problem can be remedied with the Retouch tool.

Figure 4.55

Another round 3D button.

Now you're ready to clean up the graphic. Use the Retouch tool with the following settings:

▶ Retouch Mode: Darken

▶ Size: 2

▶ Shape: Round

▶ Opacity: 50

▶ Paper Texture: None

The result will look like figure 4.56.

Tip

Save the image before applying the Retouch tool, so you can easily start over if you're unsatisfied with the results. During the retouching, if you lift the brush by releasing the mouse and then continue working on the graphic, only the most recent retouches will be affected by an Undo.

Figure 4.56

White edge retouched out.

With the Retouch tool still selected, change the Retouch Mode to Soften and smooth out the areas where the shadow became too dark during the last step (see fig. 4.57).

Figure 4.57

Final retouched button.

If the previous method seems too difficult, there is an easier option. Create another new graphic with the same dimensions. Using a

■Note

Proper retouching can often mean the difference between a professional-quality image and one that was obviously created by an amateur. Retouching isn't what is seen; rather, it is the skillful elimination of what should not be seen.

copy of the button without the shadow applied, select the white area. Then choose Selections, Invert to select the button portion. Choose Edit, Copy. Then click on the new graphic to make it the current one, and choose Edit, Paste, As New Selection, pasting it toward the bottom right. Set the foreground color to black and use the Fill tool with a high tolerance (try 150) to fill the button. Too low a tolerance will not fill the circle. Another option is to set the Match Mode to None to fill the entire selection. Your choice will depend on the contrast between the colors of the gradient fill and the background. De-select the circle with Selection, None, and then use Image, Normal Filters, Blur More a few times on the image (see fig. 4.58).

Figure 4.58

Predefined shadow.

Another Edit, Paste, As New Selection will let you place the button over the shadow. This time the antialiased line will barely be visible (see fig. 4.59). After this button has been resampled down to the appropriate size, the line won't be noticeable at all.

Figure 4.59

Completed 3D round button.

Other interesting buttons can be created by using a different variety of fills for the inner circle, as in figure 4.60.

Figure 4.60

Round 3D button created by using a Sunburst fill.

Figure 4.60 was created by using a Sunburst fill with the offset set at 70 vertical and 80 horizontal.

Figure 4.61 uses a Radial fill with both the vertical and horizontal set to 50 to give the impression of a pointed cone button.

Figure 4.61

Round 3D button created by using a Radial fill.

Oval Buttons

To achieve a beveled edge on an oval button, follow the steps used to create a beveled round button, but this time set the Selection tool to Ellipse (see fig. 4.62). Other than that, the processes are identical.

You can use the same procedures as outlined in the preceding section to create a drop shadow.

Now you'll create a non-beveled oval button.

■**Note**

Even a plain button without any bevels can appear less flat with the addition of a shadow.

Figure 4.62

Oval 3D button.

To do so, open a new 200×100 16.7 million color graphic. Use the Selection tool to draw an ellipse starting at 16,16.

Set the foreground color to black and fill the selection. De-select the selection with Selections, None. Select Image, Normal Filters, Blur More to soften the shadow. Apply the filter three or four times (see fig. 4.63).

Figure 4.63

Oval shadow.

Edit, Paste, As New Selection will place the ellipse selection over the shadow. Place it so the shadow appears around the bottom right. Select a foreground color and use the Fill tool to color the selection (see fig. 4.64).

■ **Tip** ▬▬▬▬▬▬▬

Before de-selecting the ellipse, select Edit, Copy to keep a temporary copy of the selected shape. You will then be able to paste this over the shadow later without having to re-draw it.

Figure 4.64

Simple oval placed over shadow.

Place some text on the button, as in figure 4.65.

Figure 4.65

Text added to oval button.

You now have a pretty neat-looking button that appears to stand away from the page. Part of the illusion is that the lettering seems to be cut out from the oval, making the oval appear to have depth. In Chapter 7, "Filters," I'll show you how the cutout effect was done.

Buttons can come in more than just these shapes, of course. We'll take a look at some of the ways buttons can be created as we progress through the book. In fact, buttons don't necessarily have to have text on them to get the message across.

Creating Navigation Icons

Icons are small pictures that represent something, such as an arrow that represents a direction. Instead of using the words "previous" and "next" on your buttons, an arrow that points to the left could represent "return to previous page," while one that points right could represent "go on to next page." I used the buttons shown in figures 4.66 and 4.67 on the GrafX tutorial pages to enable readers to navigate from one tutorial to the next and back again. There are other navigational buttons present as well, but I feel these two buttons clearly mean the viewer can move back and forth through the tutorials.

Figure 4.66

Round navigational button (previous).

Figure 4.67

Round navigational button (next).

If you look again at the imagemap from Chapter 2, "Color Quality," you'll notice that several other icons were used in that graphic (see fig. 4.68). The round button at the top left of the image has a house on it. This, of course, represents "Home" for home page. The button below that one has a question mark on it. This

could be used to stand-in for the word "About" or "Help." Icons can be utilized instead of text for some of the more common choices you present to your viewers.

Figure 4.68

Imagemap first seen in Chapter 2.

The advent and prevalence of Graphical User Interfaces (GUIs) has meant that computer users encounter more and more icons. Icons have actually started to be associated with the use of computers.

Part of the reason for using icons on web pages is to get a message across while using less space. A round button doesn't allow for large text, yet it can readily hold an icon. Another rationale for icons is the global aspect of the web. People who speak many different languages use the web on a daily basis. Although icons are not necessarily universal due to cultural differences, some icons are quickly becoming fairly standard. Whether someone is using Windows or a Mac in English or in some other language, the small pictures, or icons, remain the same. A picture of a disk, for example, still means "file," while two computers connected together means "network."

Some icons are easy to create. The question mark and the arrows in the image map graphic (see fig. 2.1) were created with the characters from a particular font. The question mark was, of course, the question mark, while the arrows were just the *less-than* and *greater-than* symbols. The house was created by drawing a couple of lines with the Brush tool and the Fill tool.

If you have trouble drawing some of these symbols, clip art can come in handy. When applied to your original buttons, the clip art won't necessarily have that "cloned" look. You can easily grab some clip-art images, shrink them down, and cut-and-paste them onto your buttons. If you find it necessary, you can always fill the pictures with a solid color.

It's possible to combine an icon with text, as well. Take a look at figure 4.69 for an example.

Figure 4.69

Text and icon together.

As you can see, this helps create a certain look while maintaining the readability of your graphics.

Creating 3D Buttons

The concept for the buttons in figure 4.70 came from looking at the stereo sound system that sits next to my computer. Although the real buttons gave me the idea for the three-dimensional look I wanted, they only vaguely resemble the finished design. I created these buttons for the first web page I designed, and the following tutorial shows how I created them. Although that particular site has been updated and no longer uses these buttons, they are still my favorite; in fact, you might see buttons similar to these popping up on some of the image maps in later tutorials.

To picture the 3D look, imagine the light coming in from the top left and striking a surface that curves outwards (see fig 4.70).

More of the light hits the left side of the button than the right. In addition, there will be a highlight line along the top third of the curved surface. From that highlight, the button's surface becomes progressively darker toward both the top and bottom of the curved surface.

Now that you have an idea of what the button will look like, it's time to get started. Open a new file with 100 as the width and 30 as the height. Also make sure you use 16.7 million as the color depth, so you can use the softening effect later.

Figure 4.70

Light from top left.

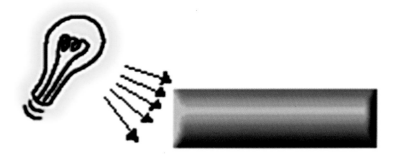

Click on the foreground color swatch to bring up the Color dialog box.

Click on the black square in the Basic Colors palette so the graduated scale along the right side of the dialog box displays a range of gray shades. Next to this scale is a small black triangle that indicates the current shade. What you'll do as you progress through creating this graphic is use differing shades of the same color.

To begin the image, choose a fairly light shade.

Now you're ready to begin drawing the button. Select the Line tool and draw two lines across the button, about a third of the way down from the top (see fig. 4.71).

Click the foreground color in the Color Swatch window again; this time when you get the Color dialog box, move the little arrow down about two graduations on the color scale to give you a little darker shade. Then draw two lines above and two more below the lines already drawn. Your graphic should now look like figure 4.72.

Continue this way, using progressively darker shades, until you've filled in the entire top third and middle of the graphic. Because you started about a third of the way from the top of the graphic there should be about a third of the image left untouched at the bottom (see fig. 4.73).

Figure 4.71

First lines, one third down from top.

Figure 4.72

Darker lines added above and below.

Figure 4.73

Two-thirds of button filled in.

Using progressively darker shades and lines that are 2 pixels wide, fill in the bottom part of the image. When you have finished, the graphic should resemble figure 4.74.

Select the Brush tool. Using the darkest shade you've chosen, draw and fill in a semicircular shape on the right side of the graphic. Then, select the Eyedropper tool and pick up the lightest shade previously used, by positioning the Eyedropper on the first lines you drew and clicking the left mouse button. Change back to the Brush tool, and draw and fill in a semicircular shape on the left side of the graphic. The result should look like figure 4.75.

Now with the power of Paint Shop Pro (and some mathematics), you'll smooth the whole graphic. Select Image, Normal Filters, Soften More. Do this twice, and your graphic should resemble figure 4.76.

Tip

Save a copy of the button before applying the text. Now all you have to do to create another copy of this button is call up the one you saved without text, and add any new text you want!

Finally you'll apply some text.

You should still have the lightest shade set as the foreground color, and you'll use this shade for the text. Select the Text tool and type some text. Select a sans serif font, set to about 16 points. If you want the text to appear to stand out from the button, select Image, Special Effects, Add Drop Shadow. Keep the vertical and horizontal numbers small—about 2 or 3— and set the blur to 0 and the opacity to 255. Voilà!!! Your finished button should look like figure 4.77.

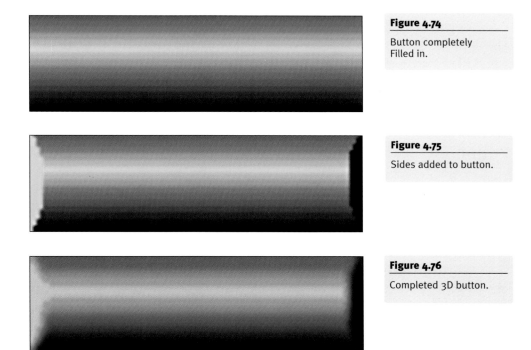

Figure 4.74

Button completely Filled in.

Figure 4.75

Sides added to button.

Figure 4.76

Completed 3D button.

Figure 4.77

Text added to 3D button.

At this point, save the graphic again, but with a new name so as not to overwrite your generic 3D button. You might want to save it as a GIF file (although saving this image as a JPG could result in a smaller, better-quality graphic). To save the image as a GIF, first decrease the color depth to 256 colors (remember, this graphic started out at 16.7 million colors). Don't worry about forgetting this step, though, as Paint Shop Pro will pop-up a message box reminding you that the color depth must be decreased before the file can be saved in the GIF format. From the main menu, select Colors, Decrease Color Depth, 256 Colors. In the dialog box that pops up, click on OK. You're now ready to save your new button. From the File menu, select Save As and select GIF as the image type. Your new button is now web-ready!

Combining Effects for a Unique 3D Button

To see how playing around with and combining some of the features of Paint Shop Pro can pay

off, take a look at another 3D button. This one's a little easier to create than the last one, yet it also has a distinctive look.

For lack of a better name I'll call this the *3D static button*. Start off by opening a new 150×50 graphic file. Set the color depth to 16.7 million.

Set the foreground color to white and the background color to black. This can be done by using the Eyedropper tool to select the white and black colors from the color swatch at the right of the Paint Shop Pro screen.

Select the Fill tool and set the Fill Style to Linear Gradient. Click on the Options button to bring up the Gradient Fill Direction dialog box. Set the Fill Direction to 115 degrees and click on OK. Click anywhere in the graphic to fill it with the linear gradient (see fig. 4.78).

Select Colors, Gray Scale. This is done so the "noise" you add to the image will be in shades of gray instead of random colors.

Figure 4.78

Linear gradient.

Select Image, Special Filters, Add Noise. Click on the Random radio button and set the %Noise to 90. Click on OK (see fig. 4.79).

Select Image, Add Borders. Click on the Symmetric check box and set the Top to 2 by entering the value or by using the spin control. With the Symmetric option on the bottom, left and right settings will now also contain the value 2. Click on OK (see fig. 4.80).

Swap the foreground and background colors by clicking on the little bent two-headed arrow at the lower left of the foreground/background color swatch. The foreground color will now be black and the background color will be white.

Bring up the Text dialog box by selecting the Text tool icon, and type some text. Don't de-select the text. Use the mouse to position the text in the center of the button (see fig. 4.81).

I used Fujiyama bold at 36 points with antialiasing on.

With the text still selected, you can now add a drop shadow. Instead of using the drop shadow effect as a drop shadow, though, you'll use it to add the effect of a highlight.

Choose Image, Special Effects, Add Drop Shadow. Set the color to white, the opacity to

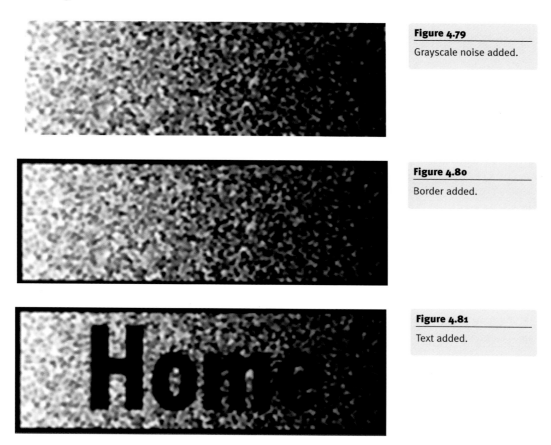

Figure 4.79
Grayscale noise added.

Figure 4.80
Border added.

Figure 4.81
Text added.

255, the blur to 0, and both the horizontal and vertical offsets to 1. Click on OK (see fig. 4.82). De-select the text with Selections, None.

See how the black text looks as though it is sunken into the button? This happens because of the white "shadow." Now you can either use the button as is, or you can choose to "colorize" it.

Choose Colors, Colorize. Set the Hue to 30 and the Saturation to 140. Click on OK to give the button a gold color (see fig. 4.83).

You can play around with the hue and saturation values to give this button an almost infinite variety of colors.

Perhaps you noticed that the Colorizing option doesn't affect the white or black areas of an image. Because of this, the text, its highlight, and the border remain unchanged. If the text had been applied to the image as a shade of dark gray (instead of black), it would have been colored gold as well. Try it and you'll see!

Additional Filters Used to Yield Marbled Appearance

To create a marbled look for this button, try applying Image, Normal Filters, Blur More once or twice before adding the border and the text. You will have to set the color depth back

Figure 4.82

White "shadow" added to create illusion of sunken text.

Figure 4.83

Button colorized to add variety.

Figure 4.84

Marbled 3D button created by using Paint Shop Pro.

Essential Elements of Your Web Page

to 16.7 million colors with Colors, Increase Color Depth first, because setting the image to grayscale will have lowered the color depth.

From figure 4.84, you can see how the simple application of one filter or effect over another creates a whole new look. In Chapter 7, we'll further explore the use of applying multiple filters.

Save this button as either a GIF or a JPG, and it will be ready to upload to your web page.

Summary

In this chapter you've built some of the basics and become more familiar with Paint Shop Pro. Now it's time to start learning some more advanced techniques.

The next chapter will cover a variety of text tricks. As you go through the techniques, though, try to think of ways to apply them to images other than just type. If you see a particular trick you like, try to imagine how else it could be used. You never know when inspiration will hit.

Chapter 5

Getting Your Message Across

In newsgroups, people often ask how to create a logo for their site. This is a difficult question to answer. I've given the matter some thought, though, and I've decided that the best approach (not to mention one of the easiest) is to stick with using text for logos. Think about it! How many corporations come to mind that have such a recognizable logo you immediately think of the company when you see it? I can think of a couple, namely Chevrolet and Nike, but it's hard to come up with many more. Most corporations use the company name or the initials as the predominant part of their logo, and for good reason. The corporation wants you, the client, to make no mistake. When you see their logo they want you to know for certain it stands for their company. This chapter discusses the use of text in the design of logos and web sites.

- ▶ Selecting a Font
- ▶ Shadowed Text
- ▶ More Shadowed Text
  - ▶ Variations on Shadowed Text
- ▶ Foreshadowing
- ▶ Reflective Text

- ▶ Gold Text
    - ▶ Deepening the Gold Color
    - ▶ Gold Text—A Different Approach
- ▶ Chrome Text
- ▶ 3D Text
- ▶ Embossed Text
    - ▶ A Simple Embossed Variation
    - ▶ A More Complex Embossed Variation
- ▶ Raised Text
    - ▶ Raised Text with Shadows and Highlights
    - ▶ Raised Text with Textures
- ▶ Easy Beveled Text
    - ▶ Shadowed and Beveled Text
- ▶ See-Through Text
- ▶ Spray (Neon Effect)
- ▶ Graffiti
    - ▶ Advanced Graffiti
- ▶ Text in a Circle
    - ▶ Variations to the Circular Path
- ▶ Opacity Effects
    - ▶ Opacity Effect Variation

Selecting a Font

Although you can't yet control which font viewers will see for the text within your web pages, you can make choices about the fonts you use for titles, logos, buttons, and such. In fact, with Microsoft Windows installed on your system, you already have a fairly wide selection of fonts available. Many peripherals and most graphics programs also come with font packages, and fonts can be found online and at your local computer store on inexpensive CD-ROMs.

In fact, this availability of fonts is what can make choosing the right one somewhat difficult. I'll present you with a few tips here and, as usual, invite you to experiment on your own.

Sometimes the font's name can help in the decision process. For example, a font like the one in figure 5.1 (Comic Sans MS) would certainly be more appropriate for a comic book site than for a business site (unless the business was a comic book or a trading card store). On

Figure 5.1

Comic Sans MS

Figure 5.2

Times New Roman

the other hand, a font like the one in figure 5.2 (Times New Roman) would look more at home on a corporate site.

Another matter to consider is the "look" of the text you'll be creating. A stone look wouldn't be easy to achieve with a slender typeface. A wooden look might be accomplished in either a slender font or a wider font. The example in figure 5.3, created with Braggadocio, might look as good in a thinner typeface as it does in the rather chunky one I've chosen.

Figure 5.3

Gold text in Braggadocio font.

On the other hand, the polished gold look might not come across as well with a more slender font.

Choices, choices! This is part of the fun of designing your own web pages and producing your own artwork. As I discussed earlier, nothing on the web is written in stone. If you don't like the look of a particular font you've chosen—change it! It's as simple as that. In fact, by keeping the filenames of your graphic images the same, all you need to do to update the title artwork on your web page is upload the new image. From that moment on, viewers will see the new look.

■**Note**

You can find a tutorial for creating this gold text in the section, "Gold Text," later in this chapter.

■**Note**

By leaving the name of your images the same, you won't have to change your HTML files. Simply uploading the new images over the old will replace the files viewers see when they load your pages.

In the following tutorials, wherever I feel it's appropriate, I'll tell you which font I've chosen, but I won't always be able to tell you why I've chosen that font. Sometimes artistic choices are made by intuition alone. As you design more logos and titles for web sites, you'll begin to get a feel for when a particular choice is working and another choice just doesn't make it.

I'll also do my best to tell you where the particular font came from—for example, whether it's a Windows font or one from CorelDRAW!— but I've installed and removed so many fonts over the years that I can't always remember where a certain font came from. This shouldn't be a problem. Many fonts are very similar, and with Paint Shop Pro you'll be able to browse through the fonts installed on your system every time you use the Text tool to enter text. If I say I've used a particular font because of a certain property (for example, the Braggadocio in figure 5.3), try to find a font that has the same properties and comes closest to matching that look.

■**Note**

Many fonts are available on the Internet. Check the Resource section for a list of some web sites where you can find downloadable fonts. Of course, by using AltaVista or some other search engine, you can find more web sites offering fonts than you can imagine.

Shadowed Text

Shadowed text is probably the most ubiquitous look on the web, as far as text is concerned. Hardly a day goes by that I don't read a post from someone in the newsgroups asking how this look can be achieved. I believe this look is popular because people want to add a certain amount of dimension to their pages. Shadowed text won't give your pages a truly 3D look, but it does make them appear less two-dimensional.

The next few examples present various ways of achieving a shadowed look. In Chapter 7, "Filters," I'll show you how to obtain a basic drop-shadow effect with a couple of mouse clicks, but for the time being, bear with me. If you find you can't achieve the look you're after by using the built-in or plug-in features—or if you find yourself using a bitmap paint program that doesn't include filters—the techniques you are learning now will be helpful.

Open a 400×200 image with the color depth set at 16.7 million colors. Set the foreground color to black, and use the Text tool to enter some text (see fig. 5.4).

The font in figure 5.4 is Brush Stroke MT. I set the size to 72 and chose Bold Italic, Antialias,

■Tip ■

Although I prefer to just make menu selections with either the mouse or the graphic tablet's pen, there are keyboard shortcuts available for many of the options in Paint Shop Pro. For example, pressing Shift-N is a quick shortcut that deselects the current selection. The shortcut keys, when available, are visible to the right of the menu selections.

Center, Floating as the options. There was no obvious reason for choosing this font. For this tutorial, just about any font will do, but brush stroke is rather elegant and is used on many web pages to good effect.

Deselect the text by choosing Selections, Select None, or by right-clicking.

Choose Image, Normal Filters, Blur More to blur the shadow text. Repeat this process until you like the look it yields. I ran the filter three times on this font (see fig. 5.5). Depending on the font you've chosen and the size of the text you've entered, you might want to experiment a little with different numbers.

After the degree of blur is to your liking, set the foreground color to the color you want to

Figure 5.4

Black text for shadow.

Shadowed Text

Figure 5.5

Blurred text for shadow.

Shadowed Text

use for the text, and choose the Text tool again to enter the text.

With the Floating option selected in the Text tool dialog box, you can accurately place the text where you want it. If you imagine the light coming from the top left, this would make the "raised" text cast its shadow to the right and down. Place the text above and to the left of the shadow to complete the illusion (see fig. 5.6).

Figure 5.6

Completed shadowed text.

The shadow behind the text makes the text appear to stand out from the page, giving the illusion that you are not looking at a flat, 2D computer screen.

I still prefer this drop shadow technique under most conditions. Not only does it give you more control over the result, but it helps you understand the underlying principles. After you understand how the shadow is cast by the light and what the result should look like, you will be able to envision variations that could not be accomplished solely through the use of filters.

More Shadowed Text

Of course, there are other ways to use light to throw a shadow from an object. Imagine the light as still coming from the top left but from a lower angle, the way it happens on a late summer afternoon. In this case, the shadow would appear to recede from the text and stretch out. You can create an effect like this within Paint Shop Pro.

To do so, open a new image file with the width and height set at 400 and 200 pixels, respectively. Start with 16.7 million colors, as always. Set the foreground color to black, and enter some text (see fig. 5.7).

Figure 5.7

Simple text in a slender font for skewing.

LONG Shadow

The Fujiyama font from the CorelDRAW! 3.0 CD-ROM is a slender sans serif font that I find appropriate with this kind of shadow effect. I set the size to 48 and chose Bold, Antialias, Center, and Floating as the options.

■Note ■

If you know your text is going to contain some characters with lowercase descenders (g, j, p, q, and y) you might want to enter the text as capitals or use another shadow method. The skewing method can be used with lowercase descenders, but there would be a lot more work involved.

Deselect the text by using Selections, Select None (or by using the shortcut Shift-N).

Now select Image, Deformation, Skew.

Set the Horizontal option to 45 (the maximum) and leave the Vertical option at 0. After running the filter three times, you should have something similar to figure 5.8.

Figure 5.8

Text after skewing.

You'll notice that the image has gained width. Now you need to crop the image to eliminate a lot of that unnecessary new background. Choose the Selection tool with the selection type set to rectangle and the Feathering option

▌Note

The Skew option will increase the size of the "canvas" (working area) of your graphic, and it will automatically use the Current Background Color (the color displayed in the lower right rectangle in the color palette at the right of the screen) for the new areas it creates. To prevent having to manually adjust the color in these new areas later on, just make sure the current background color is the same as the background of your image. You can easily set the current background color to the color of the background of your image by choosing the Eyedropper tool, moving the cursor onto the background of your graphic, and clicking the right mouse button.

set at 0. After you've made the selection (I selected an area of 500×200 around the text), choose Image, Crop to obtain a more proportioned image.

If the preceding procedure changes the zoom factor of your image, you might want to reset the view to normal with View, Normal Viewing.

You might also have noticed that the letters have picked up some aliasing. To get rid of this stairstep effect, choose Image, Normal Filters, Soften More. This will get rid of the jaggies without much image distortion (see fig. 5.9). I ran the Soften More filter twice to achieve an acceptable look for the shadow.

Figure 5.9

Text softened to remove jaggies.

Set the foreground color to the color you want to use when drawing the text, and then choose the Text tool. Position the tool carefully over the shadow, making sure the bottoms of the letters line up with the shadows (see fig. 5.10).

▌Note

I'll demonstrate a variation further on that requires figure 5.9. You might want to save the image at this point so it'll be available for you to try the variation with. Also, be sure to save the completed image in figure 5.10 with a different name so you don't write over the one you saved from figure 5.9.

Figure 5.10

Completed text with perspective (long) shadow.

Variations on Shadowed Text

It's possible to add to the illusion by making the shadow get lighter as it gets farther from the text. To accomplish this you'll need to build and use an image mask. Masks will receive more in-depth coverage (no pun intended) in Chapter 8, "Special Techniques." If you're not clear on what masks are or how they work, a quick read of that section might help.

Start out with the text version from figure 5.9. Choose Masks, New, From Image and the defaults This Window and Source Luminance.

Choose Masks, Edit to edit the mask.

Set the foreground color to black, and use the Shape tool to draw a black rectangle from the bottom of the shadow. This rectangle should fill in every part of the image below the shadow (see fig. 5.11).

Leave the foreground color as black, and set the background color to white. Choose the Selection tool, and make a rectangular selection from the upper left corner of the image to the right side of the image and as far down as the bottom of the shadow text (see fig. 5.12).

Figure 5.11

Preparing a mask, step one.

Figure 5.12

Preparing a mask, step two.

Choose the Fill tool, and set the Tolerance to 200 (the maximum) and the Fill Style to linear gradient. Click on the Options button to bring up the Gradient Fill Direction dialog box, and set the Direction option to 0 degrees.

Click the mouse anywhere in the selected area. Your screen should look something like figure 5.13.

Choose Masks, Edit to re-display your original image.

Choose Colors, Adjust, Brightness/Contrast. Set the %Contrast to 0 and the %Brightness to 100. I ran this adjustment four times to arrive at the result shown in figure 5.14.

Notice how the shadow gets lighter as it recedes, because the linear gradient mask affects how the brightness adjustment is applied. If you take another look at figure 5.13, you'll see that the gradient becomes lighter near the top of the mask. This effect determines how much the adjustment affects the image through the mask.

Now, all that's left to do is add the actual text. Choose a foreground color and use the Text tool to add the text. Position it carefully over the shadow, and you'll see how this simple change adds to the overall shadow effect (see fig. 5.15).

Figure 5.13

Completed mask.

Figure 5.14

Completed shadow variation.

Figure 5.15

Completed variation of foreshadowed text.

The illusion can be enhanced even further by applying the Blur More filter to the image through the mask. Starting with figure 5.14, choose Image, Normal Filters, Blur More and apply it several times until you're happy with the result. I ran it four times (see fig. 5.16).

figure 5.16

Shadow is blurred as well as brightened.

Notice the difference between figure 5.14 and figure 5.16. As well as getting lighter, the shadow gets softer in figure 5.16 as it recedes. After you add the text on top of figure 5.16, you should have something that looks like figure 5.17.

This final image took a fair bit of work, but I believe it was worth it—the result is a very professional-quality graphic. All that's left to do now is save the file and upload it to your web site.

Foreshadowing

Here's a shadowing trick I haven't seen used on any web pages (quick, get this one up before it's done to death).

Creating this image will take a bit of work. You won't be able to just follow along and use the same numbers I have, because this process varies widely (wildly) depending on where you place the text within the image, which font you choose, and so on. Start off by using the same numbers I do and then try playing around a little to achieve the best result you can—it'll be worth it!

In any event, I've tried to break the steps down and sequence them in a way that takes most of the guesswork out of the process.

Open a new file at 400×300×16.7 million colors. Next, set the foreground color to the color you want the text to be, choose the Text tool, and enter some text. I used the Arial font at 48 points with bold, antialias, and floating selected. Try to place the text in approximately the same position you see in figure 5.18.

Figure 5.17

Completed variation with brightening and blurring to suggest receding shadow.

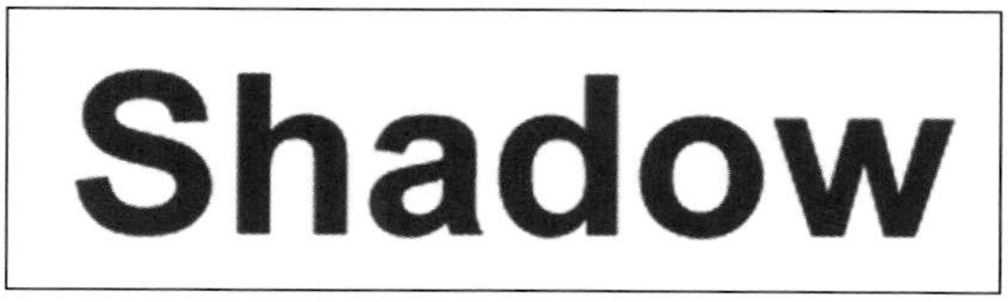

Shadow

Figure 5.18

Simple text.

Set the foreground color to black and choose the Text tool. Set the font size to 72 and then click on OK.

Choose Image, Flip to flip over the black text as shown in figure 5.19. Then deselect the text by right-clicking or choosing Selections, None.

Deselect the shadow text and then choose the Selection tool. Set the selection type to rectangle and the Feathering option to 0. Make a selection around the shadow text, starting at the left side of the graphic and as close to the bottom of the real text as you can get (see fig. 5.20).

▌Tip

Flipping the black text is necessary because a shadow placed in front of the text should, of course, be upside-down. Leave a little space between the text and the shadow for now, but not too much.

Select Image, Deformations, Perspective Vertical. The value you enter in the Percent Difference spin control will depend on the size of the selected area. You might have to try a few numbers to get it right, using Edit, Undo if what you try doesn't work.

Figure 5.19

Text with inverted copy in black.

Figure 5.20

Selected shadow text.

What you're trying to do is get the size of the top of the shadow text to match up with the size of the real text. If the shadow text is smaller than the real text, lower the spin control number. If the shadow text is larger than the real text, raise the number. In figure 5.21, the value –35 worked just fine.

Figure 5.21

Shadow with perspective.

After finding the right number for the distortion, move the selected shadow text into position under the real text.

To add to the illusion, you can add a mask to the image. Choose Masks, New, From Image and, under Source Window, select This Window.

Choose Masks, Edit.

Choose the Selection tool and then make a selection from 0,0 (the top left corner of the image) to cover the part of the image that contains the real text, not the shadowed text.

Choose the Fill tool and then set the Match mode to None or the Tolerance option to 200 (the maximum). Fill the selection with black (the current foreground color) by clicking the mouse anywhere inside the selected area. The black should totally cover the real text, as shown in figure 5.22.

Choose Selections, Invert. The bottom portion of the image (the mask, actually) is now selected.

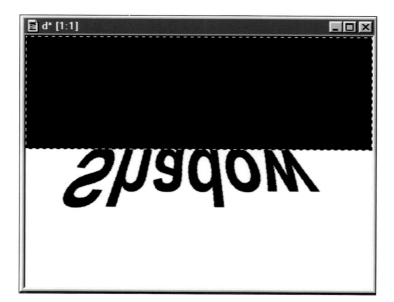

Figure 5.22

Partial mask.

If necessary, set the background color to white.

Change the fill style to linear gradient and then click on the Options button. Set the direction to 180 degrees. The gradient preview should go vertically from black at the top to white at the bottom. Click on OK.

Click the mouse anywhere in the selected area to fill that portion of the graphic with the linear gradient (see fig. 5.23).

When the mask is completed, turn the mask off by choosing Masks, Edit. The full text image should reappear.

Choose Image, Normal Filters, Blur More. Repeat this at least six or seven times.

Choose Colors, Adjust, Brightness/Contrast. Set the percent brightness to 100 and the percent contrast to 0. Click on OK. Repeat the process at least three or four times.

At this point your finished image should resemble figure 5.24. You can now crop the image and save it to use on your web site.

Reflective Text

Reflective text is as difficult to create as it is popular. In this section, I will discuss two types of reflective text, gold and chrome. Gold text is fairly popular, and there are many variations you can use to create text that appears as though it has been cast from real gold.

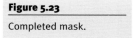

Figure 5.23

Completed mask.

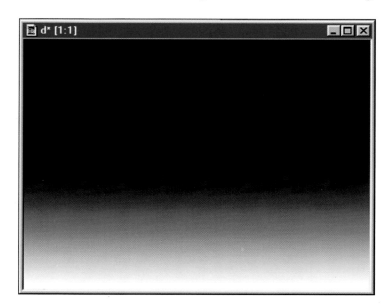

Figure 5.24

Completed foreshadowed text.

A chrome look is much harder to create. I have seen many different versions of chrome text done with higher-end programs, but I only liked a few of them. I'll present a method I've come up with that looks like chrome that is easy to accomplish in Paint Shop Pro.

Gold Text

Gold text, although it reflects its surroundings, retains some of its own yellowish color. This yellowish color can range from almost white to a yellow so dark it's almost black. The gold text tutorials below won't use this whole range of colors; they will, though, create a couple of reasonable illusions.

This first project will show you how to achieve a "gold look" for your text. I've seen many examples of this on the web, each one different from the others. As with other reflective materials, the appearance of gold can vary, depending on lighting, the surroundings, and other factors. That said, here's the interpretation.

To begin, open a new file at 16.7 million colors with the background color as similar as possible to the background color you'll be setting the "gold" text against. I'll be using white, because that's the color on which this page is printed. Next, set the graphic's dimensions to the size you need. A good starting point might be 320×85. You can adjust this size, depending on the text you need to enter and the font you'll be using.

Choose the Text tool and then type your text. I used the Scott font (at 48 points) that came with CorelDRAW! 3.0, but you can use whatever font you prefer. Make sure the Antialias and Floating options are turned on. Position the text where you want it in the graphic and then deselect it by right-clicking or choosing Selections, Select None (see fig. 5.25).

Now you're going to color the text, using the Fill tool. You'll need to select the colors first, though. I set the foreground color to a goldish yellow and the background to a reddish brown.

In this example, the yellow value is R:202 G:191 B:2 and the brown is R:141 G:84 B:7. (See Chapter 2, "Color Quality," for more information.)

You can change these colors a little, but you might want to use them as a guideline. The colors can be set by left-clicking on the Color Selection window at the right of the screen to bring up a Color dialog box. In the RGB windows, set the appropriate values.

Now, select each letter one at a time by using the Magic Wand. Make sure you have the feather value set to at least 1 to preserve the soft edges of the text (see figs. 5.26 and 5.27).

Tip

If, as in this case, not all of the letter gets selected, hold down the Shift key and select the other part(s).

GOLD TEXT

Figure 5.25

Simple text in a chunky font.

Figure 5.26

Portion of first letter selected.

Figure 5.27

All of first letter selected.

Now you can start to turn the text to gold. Click on the Fill tool and set the fill style to Linear Gradient. Then click on the Options button to bring up the Gradient Fill Direction dialog box (see fig. 5.28).

To support the illusion that the surface is reflecting its surroundings, you'll use a different fill direction for each letter. Adding 15 degrees to the direction as you fill the separate letters will work fine. To prevent the illusion from

Figure 5.28

Gradient Fill Direction dialog box.

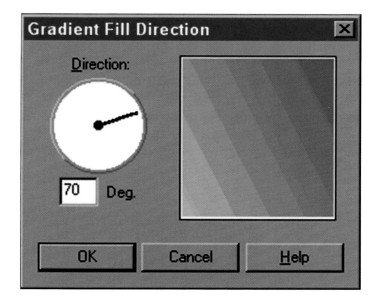

looking too static, don't use 0, 45, 90, or any other straight direction. I chose 70 degrees as a starting point. Click on OK and then click anywhere on the letter to fill all the parts of it with the gradient (see fig. 5.29).

To continue, use the Magic Wand to select the second letter, making sure you select all the different parts of the letter. Click on the Options button for the fill gradient and add 15 degrees to the direction. Fill the second letter as in figure 5.30.

■Tip■■■■■■■■■■■■■■■

Change the color resolution to 256 colors, save the graphic as a GIF with a transparent background, and it's ready to upload to your pages.

Continue selecting and filling the subsequent letters, making sure to add 15 degrees to the direction you select, until all the letters are filled.

Your finished graphic should resemble the one in figure 5.31.

Figure 5.29

First letter filled with gold gradient.

Figure 5.30

Second letter filled with gold gradient.

Figure 5.31

Finished gold text.

Deepening the Gold Color

To deepen the gold color, set the foreground color to a pale yellow. I used R:252 G:141 B:176.

Choose Image, Special Effects, Hot Wax. This effect will coat the whole image and give a beveled appearance to the text, as shown in figure 5.32.

The technique just described gives a rich look to the text as well as coloring the background. Now, leaving the foreground color set at the pale yellow, set the background color to white (or back to any other color you chose for the background of the image). To do this, choose the Color Replacer tool and double-click with the right mouse button anywhere on the background portion of the image. This sets the background color back to its original color, as shown in figure 5.33.

If any spots of yellow are left over (as in figure 5.33), choose the Brush tool, reverse the foreground and background colors by clicking on the bent two-headed arrow in the Active Colors display box, and retouch the spots. Your final image should resemble the one shown in figure 5.34.

Gold Text—A Different Approach

This last technique I'll describe for producing a gold look can be achieved quite easily. First, create a new image at 400×100×16.7 million colors. Leave the background color of the image at the default white for this effect.

Set the foreground color to R:240 G:245 B:59 (a bright yellow) and the background color to R:179 G:139 B:34 (a medium brown).

Choose the Text tool and select a really fat font. I used Braggadocio at 72 points with bold, antialias, and floating selected, as shown in figure 5.35.

Figure 5.32

Gold text with a hot wax coating.

Figure 5.33

Hot wax removed from background.

Figure 5.34

Finished gold text.

Choose the Fill tool and then set the Fill Style to Linear Gradient. Click on the options and set the direction to 180 degrees so the fill goes vertically from the yellow to the brown.

Click anywhere on the text to fill it with the gradient, as seen in figure 5.36.

Deselect the text by choosing Selections, None.

Choose the Magic Wand and set the feather value to **3**. Click anywhere on the white background to select the whole background (be sure you select any white area that might be in the center of any letters by pressing the Shift key while selecting them).

Choose Selections, Invert so the text is selected.

Choose Image, Normal Filters, Blur More and repeat the blur at least twice.

Deselect the text.

Set the foreground color to white and choose Image, Special Effects, Hot Wax. This time, because the background is the same color as the wax, the background color won't change, but you will get a nice polished gold effect on the text. With the gradient underneath the hot wax, you'll also get a reflective appearance on the bevel that appears with the application of the wax, as shown in figure 5.37.

You'll notice, too, that the bevel is wider now, due to the slight blur you put on the image.

Chrome Text

As I stated above, chrome text is much harder to create than gold text. Chrome doesn't really have a color of its own and reflects more of its surroundings than gold does.

Figure 5.35

Simple yellow text.

Figure 5.36

Text with yellow and brown gradient fill.

Figure 5.37

Completed gold text.

To achieve the following chrome look, start out with a texture for the text to reflect.

After playing around with various photos and scans, I found the best image to use was the one of the paper I had scanned in for the web page background I used for the online tutorials.

I started with a piece of paper from my printer. I crumpled it up in a ball and held it in my hand for about five minutes or so. I then flattened it gently and scanned it into the computer (see fig. 5.38). You can try this, too, if you have a scanner available, or download the file from the GrafX Design web site at `http://www.grafx-design.com`.

The resulting scan is a little too small to use for a texture for text. To get around this problem, open a new file that is 500×200×16.7 million colors. Choose the Fill tool and, under Fill Style, select Pattern. Click on Options and select the name of the paper image for New Pattern Source. Set the new image to Current and then click anywhere in the image to fill it with the paper pattern (see fig. 5.39). You might notice that the edges don't match up the way you'd want them for a background tile, but in this case, that doesn't really matter. By the time you finish, the paper texture won't resemble itself anyway.

To achieve a good chrome illusion, the crumpled paper needs to have a high contrast, but this can't be accomplished easily with the Brightness/Contrast control. Instead, choose Colors, Adjust, Gamma Correction. I used a setting of 0.30 to get the paper to resemble the image shown in figure 5.40.

Figure 5.38

Scan of crumpled paper.

Figure 5.39

Larger image filled with paper texture.

Figure 5.40

Scanned paper with Gamma adjusted to add contrast.

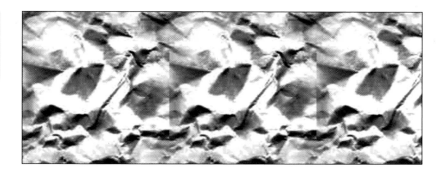

Now open another new file with the same dimensions as the last new file—this is where you'll prepare the text. Set the foreground color to black and the background color to white.

Choose the Text tool and enter some text. I'd recommend using another fat font. I used the Impact bold italic font at 72 points. Leave Antialias and Floating checked.

Deselect the text with Selections, None. Swap the foreground and background colors by clicking on the small bent two-headed arrow in the Active Colors box.

Select the whole image by choosing Selections, All. Choose Edit, Copy, and then make the texture the current image.

Choose Edit, Paste, As Transparent Selection.

Your image should now look similar to figure 5.41.

Choose Selections, Invert to select the text.

Choose Image, Normal Filters, Blur More. This will give the interior of the text a nice reflective appearance, like you can see in figure 5.42.

To complete the illusion, you can add a border. Choose Selections, Modify, Feather, and enter a value of **3** in the Feather Selection dialog box to expand the selection area around the text.

With the foreground color still set at white, choose Image, Special Effects, Hot Wax Coating. Your final result should resemble figure 5.43.

Although there were quite a few steps involved, I think the result is worth the work.

Figure 5.41

Text selection placed over texture.

Figure 5.42

Slight blur added to text.

Figure 5.43

Completed chrome text.

3D Text

If there is any type of text more sought after for web pages than text with a drop shadow, it would be 3D text. Hardly a day goes by that I don't read a post from someone wondering how they can achieve a 3D-look with their 2D paint program. Chances are they have probably seen an image similar to figure 5.44.

Unfortunately, they aren't aware that 3D images like this are created with a program designed specifically for creating 3D images. This image, for instance, was created with Simply 3D from Micrografx. Creating an image with 3D text like figure 5.44 just isn't possible with a 2D paint program such as Paint Shop Pro. You need a program that enables you to

▮Definition▮

Extruding is the process of adding depth to a two-dimensional image. After an image has been extruded, it has a third dimension that will be visible as the object is rotated in three-dimensional space.

move the text around in 3D, to apply light, shadows, textures, and colors, and to expand or "extrude" the text in all three directions.

Figure 5.45 shows yet another example of 3D text that can be found on the web. This image was created by using CorelDRAW!, an illustration program.

Figure 5.44

3D text rendered with Micrografx Simply 3D.

Figure 5.45

3D text created with CorelDRAW!

Some illustration programs, such as CorelDRAW! (used to create figure 5.45), have the capability to *extrude* text. They can then move the text around in 3D space, light the text, and cast shadows upon its various faces. Again, this type of effect is just not possible with a 2D paint program.

But don't be discouraged; until you're ready to invest in a different variety of graphics program, you can approximate 3D text. All it takes is a few clever illusions.

Start with a new 400×200×16.7 million color graphic.

To create the illusion of three dimensions, you need to give the text a top or bottom and sides. To further add to the illusion, the color of the side and top should fade as the text gets farther away. You'll need to build up the top and sides one layer at a time, starting with the layer farthest away and working up to the top layer, making each layer a little darker than the ones below it. Finally, you'll need to apply the actual text layer.

Set the foreground color to a fairly light shade of the color you have chosen. I used a light blue with R:204 G:247 B:254. When you click on the foreground color to change it, the Color dialog box appears. At the right of the dialog box is a vertical sliding scale (see fig. 5.46). For each new layer, click on the foreground color and, when the dialog box opens, drag the little black triangle slider down a couple of notches to darken the foreground color by a few shades.

Figure 5.46

Paint Shop Pro Color slider.

Choose the Text tool and type some text. I used a large font called Impact, chose the largest size (72 points), and set the style to bold. Activate the Antialias and Floating options, as well.

Type in your text. After you click on OK, the text should be ringed by the *marquee*—which looks like moving ants—signifying that you can move the text around in the image. Place the mouse over the graphic until the pointer changes to a four-headed cross. By holding down the left mouse button, you can now move the text. As you move the text around the image, take note of the x and y coordinates at the lower left of the Paint Shop Pro screen designating the x and y position of the top left corner of your selection. Move the text around until the x and y values both equal 45 and then choose Selections, None to deselect the text (see fig. 5.47).

Click on the foreground color swatch. When the Color dialog box appears, drag the slider down a couple of notches to darken the color.

Choose the Text tool again and, because the text will remain the same, just click on OK.

This time, move the text around until the x and y values both equal 46, in effect adding 1 in a horizontal and vertical offset (see fig. 5.48). This takes a little work and a steady mouse hand, but it can also improve your win/loss record at the video arcade.

Repeat the process several times, each time making the new layer a little darker and offsetting it by one pixel in both the x and y directions. After you've added a few more layers (keep going until you're satisfied with the result), you should have an image similar to the one in figure 5.49.

The preceding image has six layers, with the top left coordinates of the separate text layers ranging from 45, 45 to 50, 50. You can build up the layers as much as you want, using a smaller shift between the changes in the shades of the color. If you do so, be sure to set the last layer a bit darker than the preceding one, so it stands out sufficiently.

Although figure 5.49 doesn't approach the 3D quality of figures 5.44 and 5.45, with a bit of

Figure 5.47

First layer of 3D text.

Figure 5.48

3D text with added layer.

Figure 5.49

Completed 3D text.

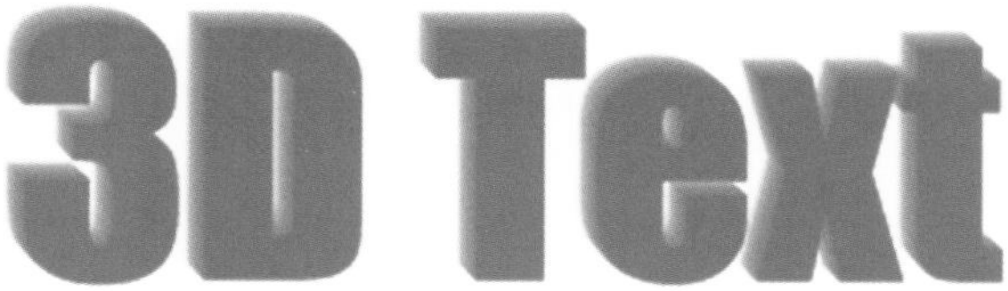

Figure 5.50

3D text with foreshadow added.

work it can become a reasonable facsimile. You can add to the illusion further by making use of the foreshadowing effect seen earlier in this chapter. You should then end up with an image similar to the one shown in figure 5.50.

You might also try filling the front of the text with a texture, or use a sunburst gradient behind the text.

Embossed Text

Another popular text look is called *embossing*. In print, embossing is the use of raised letters. You can use this effect to create a nice tiled background for your web pages that incorporates your company logo.

Paint Shop Pro has a built-in Emboss filter, but it does have its limitations. To see how this

filter works, open a new 400×200×16.7 million color graphic.

Choose the Text tool and type some text as in figure 5.51.

Figure 5.51

Simple text.

Emboss

Choose Image, Special Filters, Emboss. The result illustrates one of the shortcomings I mentioned (see fig. 5.52). During the emboss process, Paint Shop Pro has changed the colors!

Figure 5.52

Text embossed by using Emboss filter.

To help control the choice of colors, choose Colors, Grayscale. This will help a little (see fig. 5.53).

Before you try to color the image, you need to lighten it a little. The best way to do this is with the Colors, Gamma Correction option. Set the value to 2.20 to lighten the image (see fig. 5.54).

Now you're ready to apply some color. Select Color, Colorize and play around with the hue and saturation values until you see something you like in the preview window. Then click on OK to colorize the image.

To achieve the result shown in figure 5.55, I set the Hue to 105 and the Saturation to 40.

Figure 5.53

Grayscale text embossed with Emboss filter.

Figure 5.54

Embossed text lightened with Gamma correction.

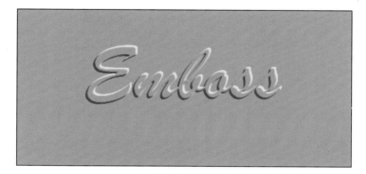

Figure 5.55

Embossed and colorized text.

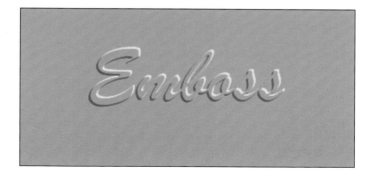

To complete the process, if you want to use this as a background tile, you might want to rotate the image, but there are a few steps to be followed before you can do that. First, set the current background color to the color of the background of the image (this is necessary because when you rotate the image, Paint Shop Pro will fill in the new information with the current background color). To do this, choose the Eyedropper tool and then right-click anywhere on the background color of the image. Second, bump the color depth back up to 16.7 million colors (it was dropped to 256 when you set the image to grayscale) by choosing Color, Increase Color Depth, 16 Million Colors. Now choose Image, Rotate and set the direction to Left. In the Degrees portion of the dialog box, choose the Free radio button and enter a value of 30 degrees.

You now have an embossed text tile you can use on your web pages (see fig. 5.56).

Figure 5.56

Rotated embossed text tile.

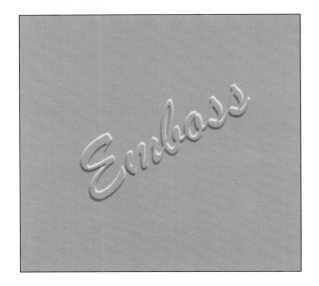

A Simple Embossed Variation

This section covers a quite popular, quick and easy method for creating an embossed look.

Start with a 400×200×16.7 million color graphic, and set the background color to white before you click on OK. Then, set the foreground color to white and enter some text by using the Text tool.

Choose Image, Special Effects, Add Drop Shadow. You might have to play around with the settings, depending on the font you choose and the size of the text you enter, so the text will be easier to read. With the right setting, you can produce a really neat effect. I've even seen this method used to display text in magazine ads and on television.

In figure 5.57, I used the Britannic Bold font set at 72 points, with Bold Italic and Antialias selected. I then used the Drop Shadow filter with the Color set to black, the Opacity set to 100, the Blur set to 20, and both the vertical and horizontal offsets set to 6.

Figure 5.57

Simple embossed text.

A More Complex Embossed Variation

The next variation yields a similar effect to that achieved with the built-in filter, but without the color shift. It just takes a little more work.

Start with a new 500×200×16.7 million color image.

Fill the image with a color (for example if you plan to set this image against a colored web page, set the background to the same color).

Set the foreground color to the same color as the background color you filled the image with. This can be done by choosing the Eyedropper tool and clicking anywhere on the image.

Choose the Text tool and enter some text (see fig. 5.58). Don't deselect the text!

Choose Image, Special Effects, Add Drop Shadow. Set the color to black, the opacity to 250, the blur to 10, and both the vertical and horizontal offsets to 3. Then click on OK.

Repeat the process, changing the color to white and the vertical and horizontal offsets to –3.

The final result should resemble figure 5.59.

Raised Text

Raised text can, in some cases, be very similar to embossed text. The difference is in the color of the text in comparison to the color of the background. Embossed text is generally the same color as the background it sits on, while raised text is a different color from its background. As with embossed text, there is more than one way to achieve a raised text look.

The first method uses Paint Shop Pro's built-in hot wax special effect.

Figure 5.58

Text with selection marquee still active.

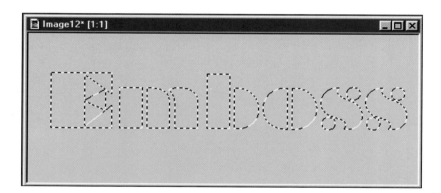

Figure 5.59

Embossed text.

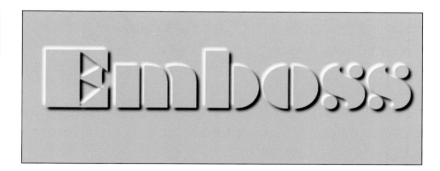

Open a new 500×200×16.7 million color image with the background color set to white.

Set the foreground color to white. Choose the Text tool and enter some text. I used the Copperplate Gothic Bold font set at 72 points, with the Style set at Bold Italic and the Antialias and Floating options selected.

Because the text is the same color as the background, all you will see is the marquee in the shape of the text, as shown in figure 5.60.

Choose Selections, Modify, Feather and enter a value of **3** in the spin box. Click on OK. This

will expand the selection a little, as well as feathering it. The difference might not be very noticeable (see fig. 5.61), but feathering the selection will change the way Paint Shop Pro applies the subsequent filters.

Choose Image, Special Effects, Hot Wax Coating. Repeat this once more to arrive at an image that should resemble figure 5.62.

Deselect the text with Selections, None and apply the hot wax coating once more (see fig. 5.63).

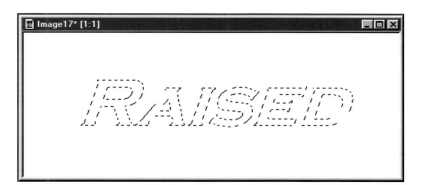

Figure 5.60

Text with selection marquee still active.

Figure 5.61

Selected text with feathering applied.

Figure 5.62

Selected text with two coats of hot wax.

Figure 5.63

Deselected text with one more coating of hot wax.

This last application of the hot wax over the whole image has added a bevel, but it has also colored the entire image. If you choose the Eyedropper tool and move it over the background of the image, you'll see the RGB numbers of the new background color displayed in the color palette. The numbers should all be 251. This means the formerly white background is now a very pale shade of gray. To change the background back to white, choose the Fill tool. As the current foreground color is still white, clicking anywhere on the background portion of the image will fill it with white. You should make sure the tolerance for the Fill tool is set to 0; otherwise, parts of the text might be affected, because the color of the text is very close to white. Also, make sure you fill in the center portions of any letters such as A or B. The final image should resemble figure 5.64.

Figure 5.64

Completed raised text.

Raised Text with Shadows and Highlights

This variation for raised text, which allows for different colors, is exactly the same as the third embossing technique, the only difference being that the text and the background can be different colors. You still shouldn't use either white or black for the text or background, because these colors will be used for the highlights and shadows, respectively.

Start with a 400×200×16.7 million color image. Set the foreground color to a medium gray and use the Fill tool to fill the image with the gray color.

Set the foreground color to the color you want for the text and, using the Text tool, type some text as in figure 5.65.

Without deselecting the text, choose Image, Special Effects, Add Drop Shadow. Set the Color to black, the Opacity to 255, the Blur to 10, and both the vertical and horizontal offset to 2. Your image should resemble figure 5.66.

Choose the drop shadow effect again. Set the color to white and add a minus sign in front of the values in both offsets (making them both −2) to achieve the final image (see fig. 5.67).

Of course, the background color doesn't have to be gray. You could use, for example, a light blue and then enter the text in a darker blue as shown in figure 5.68.

Getting Your Message Across

Figure 5.65

Simple text.

Figure 5.66

Simple text with shadow added.

Figure 5.67

Simple text with shadow and highlight added.

Figure 5.68

Simple text with shadows and highlights.

Raised Text with Textures

This last variation will describe a method for giving the appearance of raised text over a textured background. If you're using a textured background on your web pages, you'll appreciate this trick.

Load the texture file into Paint Shop Pro. I've chosen a wood texture from a photo I scanned in (see fig. 5.69).

Choose the Eyedropper tool and pick out a color that seems to be the most predominant color in the texture. The difficulty of choosing the right color can vary from texture to texture, but doing so is vital for making this illusion work.

Note

Refer to the section on "Choosing the Right Colors" in Chapter 2, "Color Quality," for a more detailed discussion on the importance of color choice.

Open a new file large enough to hold the text you want to enter, and fill the image with the color you selected with the Eyedropper. Choose the Text tool and type some text. Don't deselect the text (see fig. 5.70).

The text is the same color as the background, so all you'll see is the marquee or selection marks.

Figure 5.69

Scan of wood paneling photo.

Figure 5.70

Selected text.

Choose Image, Special Effects, Add Drop Shadow. Set the Color to black, the Opacity to 250, the Blur to 10, and both the vertical and horizontal offsets to 3. Click on OK.

Choose the drop shadow effect again and change the color to white and both offsets to –3. Click on OK. You should have a graphic that resembles figure 5.71.

If you save this file as a GIF with the Transparent option turned on and with the dominant color chosen to be transparent, the text from this image will appear to rise out of the surface of your background texture when loaded onto the your web page, as it does in figure 5.72.

Easy Beveled Text

Beveling is another ubiquitous look for graphic text on the web. In most programs, bevels would be impossible to create without the use of plug-in filters. Paint Shop Pro 4.0, though, has a built-in filter that was used in some of the previous tutorials—the Hot Wax filter.

This filter can be used for many different effects. In previous examples, we used this filter to help create gold and chrome text. In Chapter 7, I'll demonstrate another chrome effect, using only the Hot Wax filter. I highly recommend you play around with this filter whenever you have some free time. Don't hesitate to apply it many times to the same image.

Figure 5.71

Selected text with shadow and highlight added.

Figure 5.72

Textured raised text.

This effect will only work with certain fonts and fonts sizes, and the result won't truly be beveled text, but it provides a cost-effective way to add a little dimension to your text.

Open a new 400×100×16.7 million color file and leave the background color white.

Set the foreground color to a fairly dark blue. I set it to R:5 G:6 B:255.

Select the Text tool and type some text. This effect works best with a small, slim, serif font. I chose Times New Roman at 48 points, with the Style set to regular. As usual, I chose the Anti-alias and Floating options. Make sure the font you've chosen resembles the text in figure 5.73.

Before deselecting the text, choose Selections, Modify, Overall Opacity. Set the overall opacity % to 20 and click on OK.

The result should be a much paler version of the text you entered and will be similar to figure 5.74.

Deselect the text. Select the Eyedropper tool. Use it to change the current foreground color to the color of the text by moving the Eyedropper over the text and clicking the left mouse button.

Choose Image, Special Effects, Hot Wax Coating. Applying the hot wax will give the text the appearance of a bevel (see fig. 5.75).

Figure 5.73

Selected text.

Figure 5.74

Text with opacity adjusted.

Figure 5.75

Text beveled with Hot Wax filter.

If you chose a wider or larger font, the effect is more of an outline, as in figure 5.76.

You'll notice that the application of the hot wax has changed the background color. To restore the background to white, first set the current background color to white in the color swatch. Then select the Color Replacer tool and double-click the right mouse button anywhere on the background portion of the image. Your image should now look like figure 5.77.

Shadowed and Beveled Text

To give the appearance that the text is standing out from the page, you can add a drop shadow. Because you're going to be dealing with an image that has several colors in it, this will be a little tricky.

Choose the Magic Wand tool and click anywhere on the background of the image. Hold down the Shift key and click on any area inside of letters such as **B**, **e**, or **d**.

Choose Selections, Invert. This will leave the text itself selected.

Choose Image, Special Effects, Add Drop Shadow.

Set the Color to black, the Opacity to 100, the Blur to 5, the Vertical Offset to 5, and the Horizontal Offset to 3 to achieve an image similar to figure 5.78.

In Chapter 7 (in the section on plug-in filters), you'll see how beneficial add-on programs can be when it comes to adding effects such as bevels to your text!

Figure 5.76

Outlined text created with Hot Wax filter.

Figure 5.77

Completed beveled text.

Figure 5.78

Shadowed and beveled text.

See-Through Text

This next effect is considered to be an advanced text technique. With the power of Paint Shop Pro 4.0, however, I'll show you how to achieve this unique look with relatively little pain.

Part of this technique was used for the chrome text tutorial. This time you'll take the process a few steps further to achieve a really interesting look.

Open the two photo images. If they are not the same size, crop one down so both images are equal in height and width. I'll use the two fall leaves images seen in figures 5.79 and 5.80, but they wouldn't have to be similar in content.

Note the height and width of the photos and create a new image with the same dimensions. The height and width of my fall photos is 480×354, so I created a new 480×354×16.7

■Note

For this example you'll need a couple of photographs. You can either scan them in yourself or download them from somewhere on the Internet (find some by searching the web with your favorite search engine). Images are also available on many binary newsgroups on Usenet. Another alternative is image collections available on CD-ROM at your local computer store. But make sure you check for restrictions on copyrighted images—often the license will only allow you to copy it for personal use.

million color image, making sure the background color was set to white.

So you can follow along, set the foreground color to black and the background color to white. Choose the Text tool and type some text as in figure 5.81.

Figure 5.79

Yellow fall leaves.

Figure 5.80

Colorful fall leaves.

Because Paint Shop Pro will only allow the font size to go 72 points, and a much larger size is needed for this effect, do the following: With the text still selected, choose Image, Resample. In the Resample dialog box, set Custom and Maintain Aspect Ratio to **on**. Enter a number in the second small window under Custom Size. For example, to double the text size from 72 points to 144 points, enter 144 and click on OK. Because you're working with a selection (the text itself), the resampling only takes place on the text (see fig. 5.82).

Figure 5.81

Simple black text on white.

If your text isn't centered, drag it around until you have it placed in the center of the image.

The exact placement isn't important as long as all the text is visible. If the text won't fit into the image, choose Edit, Undo and set the size to a smaller value in the Resample dialog box.

Swap the foreground and background colors by clicking on the small bent two-headed arrow in the Active Colors box.

Choose Selections, Select All. Then choose Edit, Copy.

Make one of the photos the current image by clicking in its title bar. Then choose Edit, Paste, As Transparent Selection.

Position the text image over the photo so it resembles figure 5.83 and left-click to drop the selection.

Swap the foreground and background colors again (the foreground should now be black and the background should now be white).

Choose Selections, Select All. Choose Edit, Copy. Make the second photo the current image and choose Edit, Paste, As Transparent Selection. Move the text around until you're

Figure 5.82

Text enlarged by using Image, Resample.

Figure 5.83

See-through text.

satisfied with its placement and choose Selections, Select None. The result should be text drawn with the pattern of the first photo, within the second photo as in figure 5.84.

You might want to pixel-edit the antialiased pixels around the lettering to get rid of the light outline. You can accomplish this by using the Brush tool set to the Pen style option, with Size set to **1**. Leave the foreground color set to black and draw over the offending pixels. To speed up the process, you can use the Line tool to fill in the areas along the sides of letters such as F and L. Your final result should be similar to figure 5.85.

Some really nice effects can be accomplished with this technique. Play around with it and see what you can come up with.

Figure 5.84

See-through text placed on photo.

Figure 5.85

Completed see-through text.

Getting Your Message Across

Spray (Neon Effect)

This is another popular text effect and is often seen on web sites that feature science fiction themes. In fact, this effect reminds me of *The X Files* television show.

A lot of experimentation was required before I came up with a neon effect I really liked. I tried many different methods, including feathering the selection, applying the drop shadow, and other forms of trickery, but nothing yielded the haunting look of true neon I came up with in this next process. In part, the trick was finding a way to achieve varying levels of brightness within the graphic.

Open a new 400×200×16.7 million color file. In the Open File dialog box, set the background color to black.

Set the foreground color to a neon green. I used R:41 G:253 B:83.

Choose the Text tool and type some text. This effect will work best with a slim, willowy font. I used the Enviro font at 72 points, with the Style set to bold and Antialias and Floating checked. Center the text and deselect it (see fig. 5.86).

The next step is a little tedious, but will help you achieve the best effect.

Choose Image, Normal Filters, Blur More and re-apply it at least ten times—yep, ten times!

This will blur the text quite a bit, as shown in figure 5.87.

Set the foreground color to black and choose the Text tool. When the Add Text dialog box appears, click on OK to keep the same text.

Figure 5.86

Simple text in a slim font.

Figure 5.87

Text with multiple applications of the Blur More filter.

Figure 5.88

Haunting neon text.

Carefully position the new black text over the blurred green text (see fig. 5.88).

You'll notice how the green appears to be brighter in some areas and darker in others.

The only other way I've seen that lets you come close to this haunting look is with the Alien Skin plug-in filters. I'll demonstrate the Alien Skin Glow filter in Chapter 7.

Graffiti

Even if you can't draw a straight line, you can create these graffiti letters.

Open a new 400×200×16.7 million color file. Set the foreground color to a brick red-brown. I used R:202 G:67 B:2. Choose the Airbrush tool and set the Size to 200, the Shape to

Round, the Opacity to 128, and the Paper Texture to Large Bricks.

Place the mouse in the upper left corner of the graphic, press and hold down the left mouse button, and drag the mouse back and forth a couple of times while moving the cursor down the image. Try not to go over the image too many times, as this will fill in the brick pattern as the Airbrush tool lays down more color with each pass. You should end up with a brick pattern resembling the one in figure 5.89.

Choose the Text tool and type some text in a large point size. I used the Comic Sans MS font.

Center the text but don't deselect it!

Choose Selections, Save. Enter a name for the file and store it in your temporary directory

Figure 5.89

Brick pattern created with Airbrush tool.

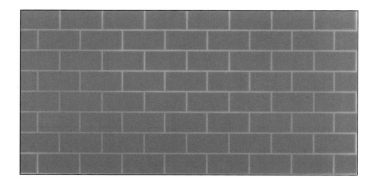

(you won't really need to keep it around after you're done with this image).

Press the Delete key to get rid of the text.

Choose Selections, Load and select the file you just saved. This will bring the empty selection, in the shape of the text you entered, into the graphic—kind of magical, eh?

Set the foreground color to whatever you prefer for the text. Then, using the Airbrush tool with the same settings, sweep the mouse over the selection while holding down the left mouse button. You'll notice how only the selected portion of the image picks up the "paint" (see fig. 5.90).

You'll also notice that the text still has the brick pattern.

Set the background color to a darker shade of whatever color you made the text and, with the text still selected, choose Image, Special Effects, Add Drop Shadow.

Set the Color option to background color, the Opacity to 255, the Blur to 15, and both the vertical and horizontal offsets to 0. This will give the text the dark outline shown in figure 5.91.

Choose Image, Special Effects, Add Drop Shadow again and change the color to black and the vertical and horizontal offsets to 5 and 3, respectively. The result will be similar to figure 5.92. Not a bad result, even if you fancy yourself graphically challenged!

Figure 5.90

Brick pattern with simple text.

Figure 5.91

Outline added to text.

Figure 5.92

Completed graffiti text.

Advanced Graffiti

If you're more artistically inclined (and if you're lucky enough to own a graphics tablet), you can try to create a more realistic graffiti effect. Start out with the brick wall (see fig. 5.89).

Select a foreground color. Then choose the Airbrush tool and set the Size to 20, the Shape to round, the Opacity to 128, and the Paper Texture to large brick.

Draw in some blocky letters by repeatedly tracing them with the airbrush until you achieve the size, shape, and look you want. I drew my name in letters with triangular shapes (see fig. 5.93).

Choose a nice bright foreground color and set the size of the airbrush to 7.

Drag the airbrush around the outside of the letters and around the inside cutouts on letters with holes. Don't worry about going for perfection here—it is graffiti after all (see fig. 5.94).

Set the foreground color to black.

Set the Size of the Airbrush to 15 and the Opacity to 70.

Draw a shadow along the right and bottom portions of the letters (see fig. 5.95).

Figure 5.93

Graffiti text created with Airbrush tool.

Figure 5.94

Outline added to text.

Figure 5.95

Shadow added to text.

If you like, you can use the airbrush to clean up the text by going over the shadow where it covers the text.

You can always zoom in to work out the finer details. What you should end up with is an image that really looks like words painted on a brick wall, as in figure 5.96.

Text in a Circle

Text in a circle—more specifically, text along a path—is a look people always seem to be after for their web sites or logos. Although the process of placing text along a path, circular or otherwise, is very easy with a vector drawing program, it cannot be performed with ease

Figure 5.96

Completed graffiti text.

when you are using a bitmap paint program. That said, there is a method that will work when using Paint Shop Pro 4.0, albeit with a bit of patience and a lot of work.

Start with a new 400×200×16.7 million color file.

Set the foreground color to a light gray (the actual color is not important, as it will only be used to draw a temporary guide).

Choose the Shape tool and set the Line to 1, the Shape option to Circle, and the Style to Outline.

Draw a fairly large circle toward the middle of the image, as shown in figure 5.97.

Choose the Magic Wand tool and set the Match Mode to RGB Value, the Tolerance to 0, and the Feather to Zero.

Click the mouse anywhere on the background of the image. Then choose Selections, Invert. Now the gray circle is selected.

After the circle has been selected, it can be moved around within the image. Move the mouse into the circle (you'll notice that the cursor changes into a four-headed arrow).

Click-and-drag the circle toward the middle bottom of the image until you have just over three quarters of the circle showing (see fig. 5.98).

You're now ready to add the text, but first you'll have to do a little arithmetic!

Count up the letters you'll be using. I entered the word "CIRCLE" (how original), which has six letters. Because you're using a semi-circle in this example, you have a total of 180 degrees to work with.

(Here comes the math part!) $180/(6-1) = 36$. Because you're actually using the spaces between the letters and not the letters themselves, you have to subtract 1 from the number of letters, so 36 is the difference in degrees you'll use as you rotate the letters.

Figure 5.97

Circular selection.

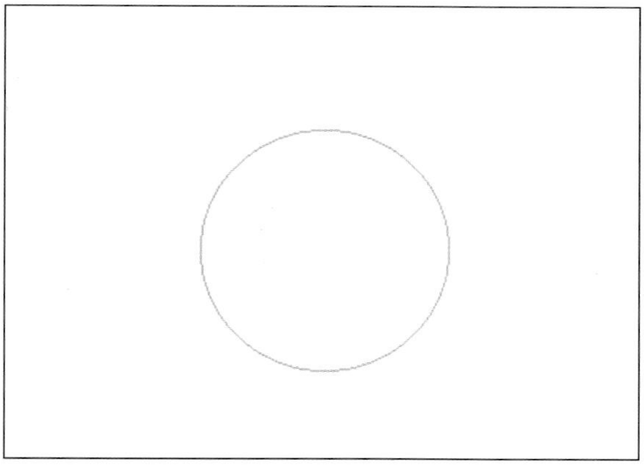

Figure 5.98

Circular selection moved to bottom of image.

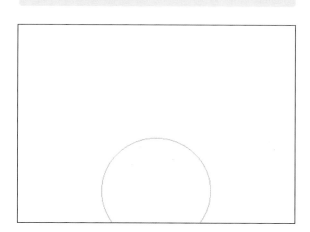

Getting Your Message Across

To further complicate the process, you can't just start anywhere and add or subtract 36. The top of the circle starts at 0 or 360, depending on how you want to count. The right side of the semi-circle is 90 and the left side is 270.

If this all seems a little confusing you might want to follow along while running Paint Shop Pro.

Now you can start to place letters. The first letter will be rotated to 270 degrees, and to each consecutive one you will add 36 degrees. Remember that when the number goes above 360, you have to subtract 360 to get the correct number of degrees to enter.

Choose a foreground color for the letters. Choose the Text tool and type the first letter. Before you deselect the letter, choose Image, Rotate and, in the Rotate dialog box, enter "right" for the direction and "free, 270" for the degrees.

Move the mouse over the letter (the cursor will turn into a four-headed arrow) and click-and-drag the letter into place near the leftmost part of the gray outline, as shown in figure 5.99.

Deselect the letter with Selections, None.

Choose the Text tool and enter the next letter. Choose Image, Rotate and add 36 to the 270 to get 306.

Place the character so its bottom makes a tangent with the gray outline (see fig. 5.100).

Rotate the next letter to 342 and set it in place.

When you add 36 to 342 for the fourth letter, you'll get a number higher than 360—372 to be exact. All you need to do is subtract 360 (372–360 = 12) and keep going.

The fourth letter is rotated to 12 degrees (see fig. 5.101).

Figure 5.99

First letter in place.

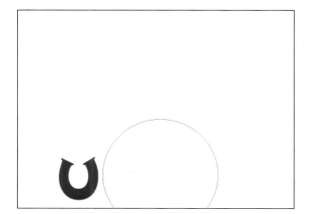

Figure 5.100

Second letter in place.

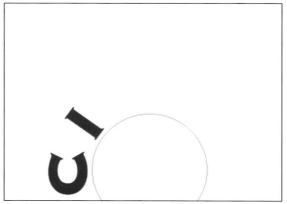

Now you can determine the attitude of the rest of the letters by simply adding 36 to the value each time you rotate a letter.

With all the letters in place, your image should be similar to the one in figure 5.102.

There are a couple of ways to get rid of the gray guideline. You can either set the Brush tool to white and draw over the outline, or you can set the foreground color to the gray of the outline with the Eyedropper, set the background color to white, choose the Color Replacer with Tolerance set to **0**, and double–right-click the mouse anywhere in the background area of the image.

If you'd like to add a drop shadow to the lettering, choose the Magic Wand and click somewhere on the background of the image (make sure the tolerance is set fairly high to combat the jaggies from the antialiased text; I set the tolerance to 100). Don't forget the letters that have holes in them—add the holes to the selection by using the Magic Wand and the Shift key. Then choose Selections, Invert and the text will be selected.

Choose Image, Special Effects, Add Drop Shadow, with the Color set to black, the Opacity set to 100, the Blur set to 15, and the vertical and horizontal offsets set to 5 and 7, respectively. Click on OK.

The final image (which took quite a bit of work, as I warned you it would) should resemble figure 5.103.

Figure 5.101

Third letter in place.

Figure 5.102

Text in a circle.

Figure 5.103

Completed text on a circular path.

Getting Your Message Across

Variations to the Circular Path

As a variation, you could start with a larger square image and use a full circle for the guideline, as in figure 5.104.

Figure 5.104

Text in a circle.

By following the steps in the previous techniques, you can place text along any path you've drawn. Of course, the math for the angles can get a little tricky. You might even try varying the size of the font of each separate letter to have the text appear to recede along the path.

Opacity Effects

While text is still selected, you can do all kinds of things to it. You've already enlarged and rotated it. You've also changed its opacity to experiment with different effects. Just using the overall opacity itself can produce some pretty neat effects.

The button shown in figure 5.105 is an example of the navigational buttons I use on my art page.

The background of the button contains various words representing the different types of art displayed on my art pages. The words were separately blurred, rotated, and set to various opacities. Then each button had a different title placed on it.

To get an idea of how the opacity feature works, open a 400×400×16.7 million color image.

Figure 5.105

Navigational button from www.accent.net/tmc/artpage.htm.

Set the foreground color to the color you want the text to be.

Choose the Text tool and type some text.

Before you deselect the text, choose Image, Rotate. Set the direction to left and the degrees to 90.

Choose Selections, Modify, Overall Opacity and set the overall opacity % to 10.

Move the text to the left side of the image and deselect it with Selections, None (see fig. 5.106).

Choose the Text tool again and click on OK to keep the same text.

Before deselecting the text, rotate it 80 degrees to the left and change its opacity to 20 (notice how, each time we add text, the two numbers add up to 100).

Place the text so its first letter matches up with the first letter of the previous text, as shown in figure 5.107.

Keep adding text, subtracting 10 from the rotation and adding 10 to the opacity each time until, finally, the last text gets placed into the image with no rotation and no change in opacity. This final image will resemble figure 5.108.

Figure 5.106

Opacity effect, step one.

Figure 5.107

Opacity effect, step two.

Figure 5.108

Completed opacity effect text.

Opacity Effect Variation

There are many variations you can achieve with opacity, but I'll leave you with this one teaser (see fig. 5.109).

To accomplish this effect, open a photo file and start a new image.

In the new image, place black text over a white background.

Select the entire image with Selections, All. Choose Selections, Modify, Overall Opacity and set the opacity to 20 %.

Choose Edit, Copy.

Make the photo the current image and choose Image, Paste, As New Selection and move the text into place. That's it!

Summary

As you can see, there are many variations and possibilities available when manipulating text for your web pages with Paint Shop Pro. Readers of my web site sometimes surprise me with variations on my online tutorials that I never thought of. The key to coming up with some new look for the title of your web page is to play around with the program as much as you can. Any time you spend learning the filters and options will eventually pay off in truly original graphics.

Now that you've created that killer logo, it's time to build a worthy background. The next chapter will cover some of the methods you can use to create seamless tiles and edge borders for your web pages.

Chapter 6

Backgrounds and Borders

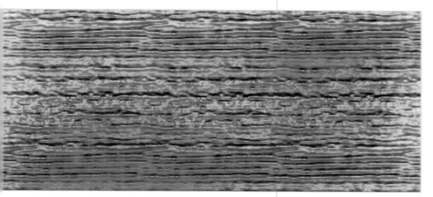

Although not all webmasters use backgrounds or borders on their pages, there are a substantial number of web sites, both amateur and professional, that put these options to good use.

There are many styles of backgrounds and borders that can help your web site stand out from the crowd. As usual, I recommend that you try some of the examples presented here, and then experiment to come up with a look that will set your site apart from others.

The following topics will be covered:

► Working with Backgrounds and Borders

► Creating Seamless Tiles

► Building Backgrounds from Logos

► Creating Great Background Textures

> ► Natural Backgrounds

> ► Homemade Backgrounds

> ► Geometric Backgrounds

> ► Wild Backgrounds

> ► Embossed Backgrounds

> ► Gradient Backgrounds

- ▶ Designing Edge Borders
- ▶ Creating Shadowed Borders
  - ▶ Torn Paper Borders
  - ▶ Artistic Borders
- ▶ Using Cheats (Built-in Texture Tools)

Working with Backgrounds and Borders

Backgrounds and borders are a pretty hot topic on the Internet. In fact, backgrounds have even become something of a commodity, with web sites springing up daily whose sole purpose is to develop and distribute seamless background tiles. One of these—located at http://www.dsb.com/play/playruff.html on the web (incidentally, dsb.com is the home of a set of plug-in filters as well)—will actually design a tile for you while you wait! This phenomenon is not restricted to amateur sites, either. Fractal

Design, (http://www.fractal.com) the designers of Painter, have a "tile of the day" on their site that you can copy with a click of the mouse.

Backgrounds, which range from artistic to distracting, can help set a particular mood for a web site. Rather than have your visitors reminded that they are indeed sitting in front of their CRTs, you can give them the illusion of holding a book or a newspaper in their hands, for example. You can use natural-looking materials such as paper, wood, or leather to help with the illusion. And filling a web page with seamless tiles is not the only option—edge borders are becoming a very popular alternative to backgrounds.

In fact, borders have gained so much in popularity that they are heavily used on many professional pages. The borders are often integrated with a set of navigational buttons to complete a certain look. The screen capture in figure 6.1 shows the gold buttons and vertical bars used at the "Powered by GrafX Design" web site.

Figure 6.1

Early version of Powered by GrafX Design home page.

One type of background you might want to avoid is something so "busy" that your text is unreadable. If your pages have a lot of text, make sure the text is indeed readable. This is not to say that busy, flamboyant backgrounds never work, just that you should be aware of the overall content of your pages. If your pages contain many graphics and buttons, for example, that would be highlighted by a colorful textured background, then by all means use one.

The gold buttons appear to be attached to the vertical bars rather than just hanging in mid-air. These elements all tie together with the gold GrafX logo to give the site an award-winning look and feel. What makes a design a winner is hard to say—like asking what is the perfect color. The following sections will describe how you can design and create your own backgrounds and borders.

Creating Seamless Tiles

We'll cover the new built-in seamless tile feature of Paint Shop Pro 4.0 in the "Using Cheats" section of this chapter. (Although the feature is fairly easy to use, it has certain shortcomings.) To begin with, I'll show you the old-fashioned way of creating tiles for backgrounds.

Start with a 200×200×16.7 million color graphic. This size tile is large enough to allow you to achieve a nonrepetitive look, yet small enough to load fairly quickly. Sketch a pattern as I've done here. (I won't be drawing anything

elaborate, just some squiggles of various lengths, colors, and thicknesses. The purpose of this lesson is to clearly demonstrate the concept behind seamless tile creation, not to produce fine art.)

Figure 6.2

Yep, pretty snazzy! Kind of Picasso-ish.

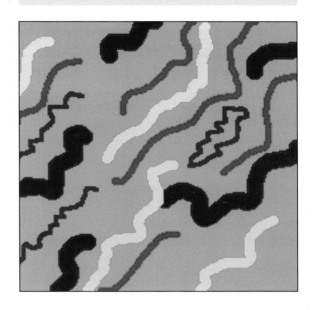

Fill your new graphic with a color and then draw some assorted squiggles on it. Figure 6.2 shows the masterpiece I came up with.

Now, cut the graphic into four separate squares and swap each square with its diagonal counterpart. Suppose you numbered the four squares that make up this graphic like the way they're numbered in figure 6.3.

Figure 6.3

Original placement of image's quadrants.

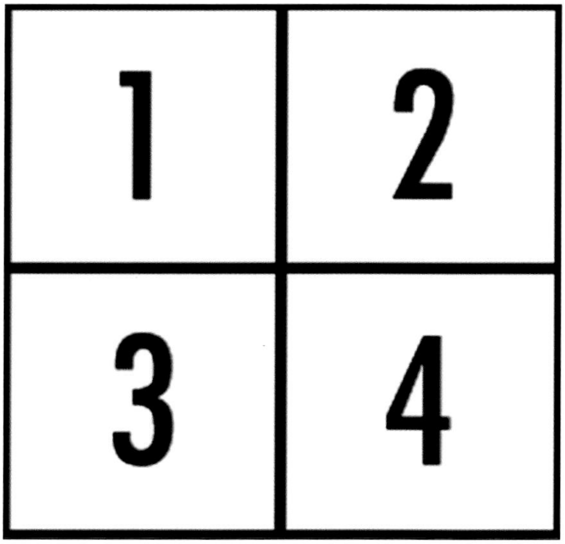

Figure 6.4

Placement of image's quadrants enabling seamless tiling.

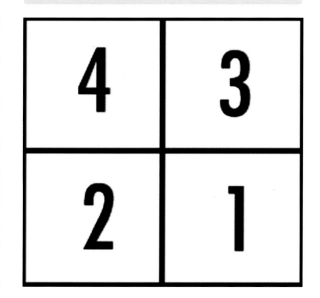

What you want to do is swap the corners diagonally. In other words, you need to switch blocks 1 and 4 with each other and blocks 3 and 2 with each other, so it looks like figure 6.4.

This is, of course, a little tricky. The first thing you'll want to do is save the image you're working on in case you mess it up a little.

Create another new graphic with the same dimensions. In this case you should create a new 200×200×16.7 million color empty graphic. This is where you'll place the squares you copy from the original.

When that's done you can begin the serious work. Select the Selection tool. Set the

Selection type to rectangle and the Feather option to 0. Place the cursor at the center of your original graphic. Remember, computers start counting at zero, not at one. This means the center of your 200×200 graphic is at (99, 99), *not* (100, 100). With the cursor placed at the center, hold down the left mouse button and drag the cursor up to the upper left corner of the graphic to select portion #1.

Choose Edit, Copy to copy your selection, switch to the new graphic (the empty one), and choose Edit, Paste, As New Selection. Move the selection to the lower right and click the left mouse button. It should look something like figure 6.5.

Figure 6.5

Top left corner moved to bottom right.

Figure 6.6

Bottom right corner moved to top left.

The border on figure 6.5 is shown here for clarity only; it won't appear in your graphic.

Now, copy square number 4 into position number 1. Re-select the original graphic, place the cursor at the center, click the left mouse button, and drag the cursor to the bottom right of the graphic. Choose Edit, Copy. Then click on the new graphic and choose Edit, Paste, As New Selection. Position the selection in the upper left corner as in figure 6.6.

You can then move square number 2 into position number 3, and square number 3 into position number 2. All of this moving is done, as above, by clicking on the original graphic, selecting the square from the 99, 99 position, clicking on the new graphic, and pasting the selection into position.

It's a bit of work, but you are left with a graphic that will tile perfectly after you follow the next few steps (see fig. 6.7).

Figure 6.7

All corners moved to new positions.

Notice the mismatched lines in the center of
figure 6.7. In this case, it was a relatively simple
task to tidy them up. I just used the
Eyedropper tool to pick up a color and then
used the Pen tool to join some of the squiggles
until I was happy with the result.

Depending on the complexity of the graphic
you have chosen to work with, this might be
harder or easier to accomplish. You might even
have to use the Cloning tool. Just be sure you
don't make any changes to the edges of your
tile. My final graphic looks like figure 6.8.

Figure 6.8

Finished tile.

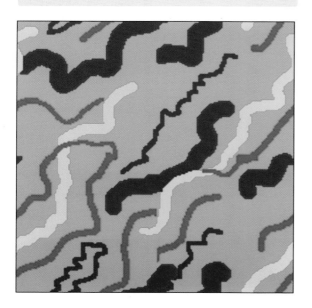

You can see that the center doesn't have any
obvious mismatched lines now.

To save room, I'll shrink the graphic to 50×50
before showing you what it looks like when
tiled. Figure 6.9 shows a background graphic
that is 4 tiles tall and 4 tiles wide (for a total
of 16) of our finished tiles.

Figure 6.9

Sample background tiled with Picasso-ish graphic.

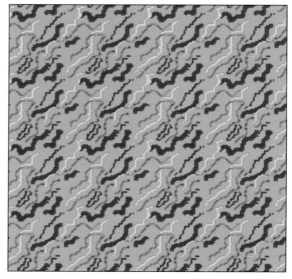

■ Note ■■■■■■■■■■■■■■

If you do make any changes to the edges of the
new graphic, it will no longer tile correctly. This
is the reason behind saving an intermediate
copy. If you mistakenly change the edges of the
tile, you might be better off opening the saved
file and starting the final touch-ups again.

Although this example isn't high art, you can plainly see that the tiles do indeed match up. Save your final graphic as either a JPG or a GIF and you can use it to tile your web pages.

Now that you have the basic tools in hand for creating seamless tiles, you can try out a few ideas.

Building Backgrounds from Logos

Even with a design you'd think wouldn't need tiling, you can use the preceding method to give your backgrounds a more dynamic look.

For example, if you were to take a company logo and just tile it for the background of your web pages, you'd end up with a static-looking page (see fig. 6.10).

Figure 6.10

Static logo background.

Compare figure 6.10 to figure 6.11.

Figure 6.11

More dynamic logo background.

Notice how the logos in figure 6.11 are placed on a diagonal? This trick, used in photography to make static subjects look more dynamic, also works well here.

Creating this final background is fairly easy, with just a step or two added to the seamless tile process described in the previous section.

Start with a logo, either hand-drawn or scanned in. I used a new GrafX Design idea I've been playing with. I converted the image to grayscale, used Image, Special Filters, Emboss, and then ran Colors, Adjust, Gamma Correction on the image to lighten it and decrease the contrast.

After I had the logo in the final version I wanted (see fig. 6.12), I was ready to tile it.

Figure 6.12

Embossed grayscale version of GrafX Design logo.

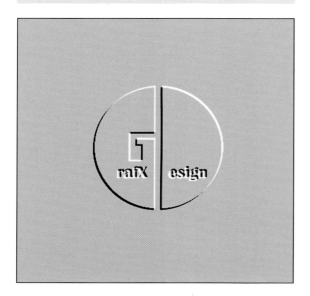

Figure 6.13

Logo graphic after rearranging the quadrants.

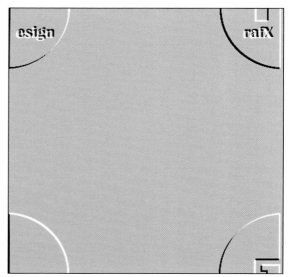

I used the steps outlined in the seamless tile section to arrive at figure 6.13.

The additional step needed here, after you've finished the tiling process, is to cut and paste the logo from the original image into the center of the new file. This will leave you with a tile, like that in figure 6.14, which can be used for the background of your web pages.

To see what this final tile will look like on a web page, I created a new file that was 1200×1200 and used the Fill tool to "paint" the tile into the image.

To fill the new image with your tile pattern, choose the Fill tool and set the Fill Style to Pattern. Click on the Options button. When the Define New Pattern dialog box opens, select the image you want to use as a fill pattern under New Pattern Source.

Figure 6.14

Final logo tile.

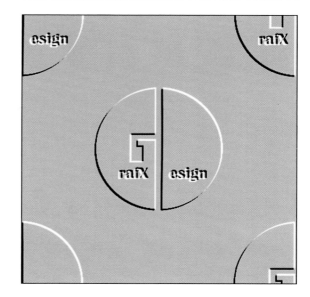

Adding an imagemap (with cut-and-paste) gave me a good idea what the final web page would look like (see fig. 6.15).

Figure 6.15

Idea for GrafX Design home page.

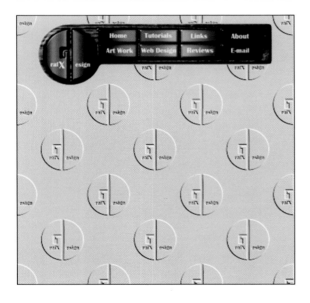

Creating Great Background Textures

Textures are another favorite for background tiles. You can get textures in all sorts of shapes and sizes, ranging from "natural" to homemade and from gradient fills to wild designs. Since the advent of the web, many texture image files are already set up for tiling. These images won't need to be processed by using the previous method, as something similar has already been done to them to make them tile-ready.

If you don't have the means to create or photograph and scan your own tiles, you can find them on the Internet (using one of the popular search engines) or purchase them on CD-ROM.

The overall theme of your web site will help you determine the particular type of textured tile you want to put up—natural, homemade, geometric, wild, embossed, or gradient.

Natural Backgrounds

Natural tiles are available from a wide range of sources. They can be found on the web, purchased on CD-ROM, or scanned in from photos. They even come as extras now with many graphics software packages.

Many patterns exist in nature that are suitable for web backgrounds. To name a few:

- ▶ Wood grain
- ▶ Plants
- ▶ Flowers

- ▶ Rocks
- ▶ Marble
- ▶ Granite
- ▶ Clouds

If you come across that perfect image for your web pages and find it doesn't become seamless when tiled as a background, follow the steps outlined in the seamless background tutorial earlier in this chapter. Although some images will be fairly easy to process, others are nearly impossible. You won't necessarily know until you try.

To see if an image can be tiled, open the image in Paint Shop Pro, and then open a larger new image whose dimensions are a multiple of the texture file.

I opened the following image in Paint Shop Pro (see fig. 6.16).

I created this wood pattern one day while playing around with Paint Shop Pro just after I first downloaded the shareware version. I was playing with some of the new features, such as Hot Wax Coating, and some of the distortions, such as Wind. Although this is not a "real" wood pattern, it'll stand in nicely for this demonstration.

If you take this texture and try to tile it, you'll get something like figure 6.17.

Although this texture tiles nicely on the vertical, it doesn't tile very well horizontally; you can see an obvious seam down the center of figure 6.17.

Figure 6.16

Wood grain pattern created with Paint Shop Pro.

Figure 6.17

Mismatched wood grain tile.

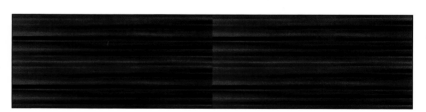

If you take figure 6.16, though, and run it through the process of relocating the corners to create a seamless tile, you'll be left with figure 6.18.

Although to the naked eye, figure 6.18 looks like a smaller version of figure 6.17, it is actually figure 6.16 after it has been run through the seamless tile cut-and-paste process, and is now ready for retouching.

Use the Retouch tool, with the Retouch mode set to Lighten, Darken, and Smudge, and run the tool over the seam in the middle of the wood grain image. With some patience, you can obtain a graphic that resembles figure 6.19.

Practice and experiment until you get an effect you like.

When this version of the wood grain pattern is tiled, as in figure 6.20, the seams match up well and the texture can be used to create an effective seamless tile background.

The same effect can be achieved with any natural pattern.

Homemade Backgrounds

Homemade patterns work just as well as natural patterns for background tiles. Patterns you might want to try include the following:

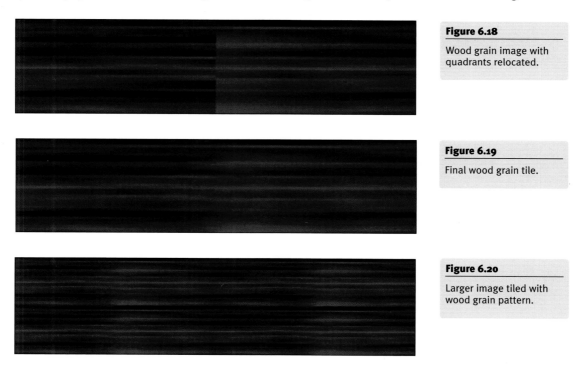

Figure 6.18

Wood grain image with quadrants relocated.

Figure 6.19

Final wood grain tile.

Figure 6.20

Larger image tiled with wood grain pattern.

- ▶ Bricks
- ▶ Window panes
- ▶ Close-ups of high-rise buildings
- ▶ Cement blocks

Homemade patterns can be rendered in 3D programs, scanned in from photos or real life, or artificially created in Paint Shop Pro. The brick pattern (see fig. 6.21) used in the graffiti text tutorial is one texture that can be created easily in Paint Shop Pro. After creating the pattern, use the process described in the seamless tile tutorial at the beginning of this chapter to create a brick tile for your web pages.

Geometric Backgrounds

Geometric patterns can be found everywhere in natural and homemade images. Bee hives are an example of patterns in nature, as are snowflakes and crystal formations. Using Paint Shop Pro and a little imagination, it is fairly easy to come up with your own geometric tiles. The tile in figure 6.22 was created by using the Paintbrush tool with the brush size set at 200 (very large) and the paper texture option set to Daze. I chose a bright red color and swept the brush

across an empty image a couple of times. I then set the foreground color to white and applied the hot wax coating.

Figure 6.22

Geometric pattern created with Paint Shop Pro.

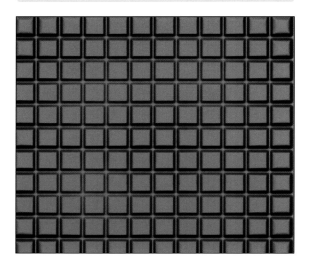

Although this particular pattern is rather bland, it does show how easy it is to create patterns with Paint Shop Pro. This image took all of two or three minutes to make.

Figure 6.21

Brick pattern created with Airbrush tool.

Wild Backgrounds

Using wild patterns is a fun way to liven up your web site. Creating a wild pattern is also a great way to loosen up and prepare yourself for more serious drawing, so relax and let your imagination go!

Open a new file and select a color. Draw some squiggly lines, change colors, draw some more. Select a different size or style for the Brush tool and continue to draw. Use a different paper texture. Some really interesting patterns will form as you play with the various tools and options. Use this warming-up period as a way to explore some of the built-in filters such as Image, Deformations, Wind or Image, Special Effects, Hot Wax Coating. Try changing the foreground color before applying the wax. If you don't like the results, simply choose Edit, Undo and try something else. This type of random play is a terrific way to learn about the power of Paint Shop Pro.

I created the graphic in figure 6.23 one afternoon while I was exploring paper textures and hot wax coatings in Paint Shop Pro.

Some patterns, such as the one in figure 6.23, might not be suitable for a background tile. As it stands, this image is a little busy and could prevent text placed on it from being readable. Wild graphics sure are fun to create, though, and can be a big help when you are learning to use the myriad (and not always obvious) features of Paint Shop Pro.

On the other hand, a pattern like this might be a good candidate for an edge border. See the section on "Edge Borders" later in this chapter for more information.

Embossed Backgrounds

Embossing is not only useful for turning your company logo into a tile background; this technique can also be used to create interesting background patterns. Creating an embossed background is really easy!

For example, take the paper background used to create the chrome text in figure 5.38 of Chapter 5, "Getting Your Message Across." By increasing the contrast and running the Emboss filter (Image, Special Filters, Emboss), you'll end up with something like figure 6.24.

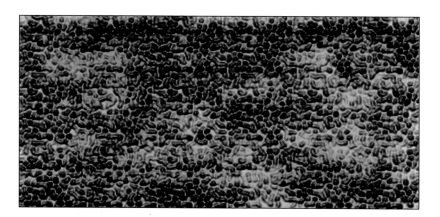

Figure 6.23

Wild pattern created while "playing" with Paint Shop Pro.

Figure 6.24

Paper texture with contrast increased and emboss filter applied.

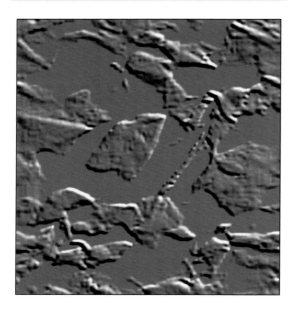

Figure 6.25

Gamma corrected to brighten and lower contrast.

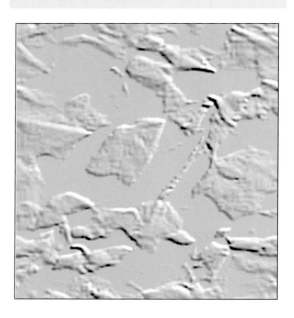

Although the pattern is still fairly busy, this can easily be corrected with Colors, Adjust, Gamma Correction. Figure 6.25 shows the result after I applied the gamma correction with a setting of 3.00.

You could also colorize the tile to make it look better in combination with your logo and buttons. Figure 6.26 shows the result of applying Colors, Colorize, with the hue set to 30 and the saturation set to 112.

Figure 6.26

Colorized version of embossed computer paper.

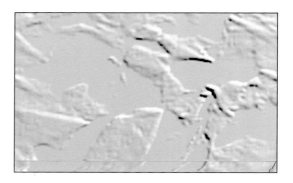

■Definition ■■■■■■■■■■■

Gamma refers to a computer monitor's brightness and contrast. After an image has been scanned into the computer, you can adjust the image's gamma. This combines the brightness and contrast adjustments and is much easier to apply.

Not bad for an image that began life as a scan of some crumpled computer paper.

Another idea would be to take the brick pattern created earlier in this chapter and, by converting it to grayscale (Colors, Grayscale) and running the Emboss filter on it, arrive at something like figure 6.27.

Again, this image could be colorized or lightened before it is turned into a tile. The possibilities are really limitless.

Gradient Backgrounds

A while back, I used a black-to-royal-blue gradient fill for the first Earth Orbit Consulting site. At the time I didn't have the latest version of Paint Shop Pro, and the higher-end graphics programs I had didn't have the capability to do gradient fills. So I painstakingly filled a long, narrow image with lines, changing the shade and color as I worked. I think that particular gradient took me the better part of a morning to create (oh, what I'll do in the name of art). Thank goodness such a blood-and-sweat method is no longer necessary!

I'll now show you how to achieve the same look in a matter of minutes.

Open a new 255×10×16.7 million color image. Set the foreground color to black and the background color to a nice rich dark blue.

Choose the Fill tool and set the fill style to linear gradient. Click on the Options button and set the direction in the Gradient Fill Direction dialog box to 90 degrees.

Click on OK. Then position the cursor anywhere in the image and left-click. The result should look like figure 6.28.

Create another new image with the height set at 10 but with the width set to 1200 pixels. Leave the color depth set to 16.7 million.

Now swap the foreground and background colors by clicking on the bent two-headed arrow in the foreground/background color swatch.

Figure 6.27

Embossed grayscale image of brick pattern.

Figure 6.28

Black-to-blue horizontal gradient.

Note

The width should be set to 1200 pixels so the image won't actually tile on your web pages. Instead, the background image will flow down the page, resembling a border more than a background tile. We'll examine this topic more in the upcoming section on borders. The 10-pixel height was selected here so the resulting image would be more visible on the printed page before tiling it. In actuality you can get away with an image as small as 5 pixels high, which results in a very small image size that will load quickly. Going much smaller can cause problems with graphics programs not wanting to write (save) the file to disk.

Choose the Fill tool and set the fill style to solid color.

Click anywhere in the new graphic to fill it with the blue.

Make the gradient image current and choose Selections, Select All.

Choose Edit, Copy. Make the blue image current and choose Edit, Paste, Paste as New Selection. Position the selection at the left of the image so you get something similar to figure 6.29.

You might want to zoom-in the new image to make the pasting procedure easier.

I've actually cropped this image down to 500×10 so it will fit on the page, but you can still see how this gradient would look. The image in figure 6.30 illustrates what this background looked like with the Earth Orbit logo in place. (The tiling is done in HTML.)

Figure 6.29

Linear gradient tile.

Figure 6.30

Original Earth Orbit Consulting background and logo.

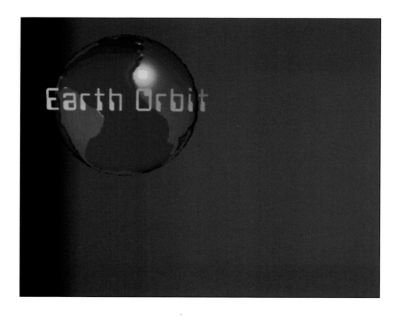

Of course, you can use any color combination for the gradient, choosing a set of colors that goes with the theme of your site and with the graphics you'll be displaying.

I chose black and blue to represent space and to go with the colors I had chosen for rendering the Earth Orbit globe.

Designing Edge Borders

Edge borders have become very popular, offering a look that can be almost as clean as a plain background. They also allow for easier displaying and readability of text and, as you can see from figure 6.1, can actually help tie a page together. All sorts of designs, from the very simple to the extremely elaborate, can be used as borders.

Keep in mind that you'll want the image to be wide enough not to tile in any pattern except vertically. Although you might be working and

designing on a system that has a 640×480 display, some of your viewers will be looking at the web on systems with displays of 1024×768 or wider! By going with 1200 pixels as stated earlier, you'll be okay.

To be safe, you should consider making your border images at least 1200 pixels wide. This should help avoid the repeating column problem that can occur when someone's display is wider than your border image (see fig. 6.31).

A solid-color border is the easiest to create. Simply open a new 1200×5×16 color image.

▌Note ▬▬▬▬▬▬▬▬

In the preceding example, creating a 1200×5×16 color image is not a mistake! Using a really small number like 16 instead of 16.7 million for the color depth decreases the final image size. Because you're only using one solid color on top of another, there's no reason to keep the color depth high.

Figure 6.31

Improper tiling due to narrow tile graphic.

Choose a color for the border and use the Brush tool to draw a line from the left of the image as wide as you'd like the border to be. The border in figure 6.32 is 60 pixels wide.

Once again I've cropped this image in width and given it a little more height to fit it to the printed page and give it good visibility. The image is now ready to use as a background tile; due to its length, this image will only tile vertically, thereby giving the effect of an edge border.

Creating Shadowed Borders

Adding a shadow to a solid-color border is a simple procedure that adds depth to the resulting image.

Using figure 6.32 as a reference, increase the color depth with Colors, Increase Color Depth, 16.7 Million Colors.

Select the red portion of the image with the Magic Wand tool.

Choose Image, Special Effects, Add Drop Shadow.

Set the Color to Black, the Opacity to 100, the Blur to 15, the Vertical Offset to 0, and the

Horizontal Offset to 7 to obtain a result like the image in figure 6.33. Experiment with the settings to get one you like (too dark a shadow at this point would just resemble stripes, though).

This border will appear very similar to the one used by JASC Inc (the people who wrote Paint Shop Pro) on their web site (http://www. jasc.com). I've seen similar simple and elegant borders used on many professional sites.

Torn Paper Borders

The question "How can I simulate torn paper?" shows up on the graphics newsgroups almost as often as the shadowed text questions. The following example is one way of achieving that look.

Start with a 300×150 graphic with the color depth set to 16.7 million. After choosing a parchment-like beige color (R:247, G:222, B:173) for the foreground, I used the Brush tool with the type set to Pen to draw a squiggly line down the graphic, starting at coordinates close to 120, 0 (see fig. 6.34).

Keeping the same foreground color, I used the Fill/Paint tool to fill in the left side of the graphic (see fig. 6.35).

Figure 6.32

Solid-color border.

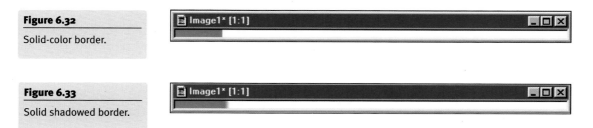

Figure 6.33

Solid shadowed border.

Figure 6.34

Figure 6.35

After using Image, Normal Filters, Blur More a couple of times, the graphic should look like figure 6.36.

Now you have to make sure the bottom and top of the graphic will line up when it is tiled down the side of a web page. You can do this by cutting the graphic in half, horizontally, and then swapping the bottom and top pieces.

■Note

Lining up the tiles in a two-piece background is the same as lining up the tiles in a four-piece tile. The only difference is you swap only the top and bottom halves of the graphic instead of the four quarters.

Figure 6.36

Choose the Selection tool and place the cursor at the 0, 0 position (upper left corner) of your graphic. Click and drag the mouse to 299, 74 (middle right side).

Choose Edit, Cut.

Open a new graphic at 1200, 150. You'll notice that, as described above, the height remains the same but the width is greatly increased. This is so the finished graphic will stay to the left when you use it as a tiled background.

Choose Edit, Paste as New Selection. Place the piece you cut from the first graphic, making sure it fits snugly into the bottom left corner of the new graphic. You might have to play with

this a bit to get it right—I did! You can use the x and y coordinate numbers at the bottom left of the Paint Shop Pro window to help you (see fig. 6.37).

After the cut piece is placed correctly, click on the first graphic to make it current. Then use Selections, Invert to select the bottom part, which was left behind from the last Edit, Cut procedure.

Choose Edit, Cut again and then reselect the new graphic and choose Edit, Paste, Paste as New Selection. Place this portion just above the last selection, making sure it fits snugly up against the bottom piece and against the left side of the graphic.

Figure 6.37

Repositioning the top half to create seamless border tile.

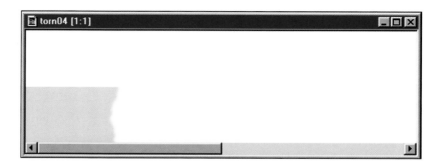

Chapter 6

Backgrounds and Borders

You will, quite possibly, notice a spot that doesn't quite line up in the middle of the parchment. That's okay—it's easy to take care of. Select the Smooth tool and rub it around the middle part where the parchment doesn't line up. Do this until the line blends in well with the rest of the edge.

To add a little realism (or the illusion thereof), you can add a little text to the parchment. To do so, first click on the foreground color swatch. When the Color dialog box comes up, keep the same shade but set the color a little darker. Mine came out as R:238, G:184, B:83.

Using the Text tool, select Times New Roman at 8 points and type 12 lines of text. You can type anything you want, but keep the lines short, about 20 characters or so. It won't be readable so it doesn't matter too much what you write.

Center the text in the parchment part of the graphic to arrive at the final version as seen in figure 6.38.

When tiled down the side of your web page, this image will resemble torn paper or parchment.

Artistic Borders

There are many ways to make an artistic and attractive edge border for your web pages. This technique will describe the steps I took to create a border for a movie review page.

Because this border was to be for a movie review web site, I chose to use a movie theme. I wanted the border to look like a strip of movie film and felt I needed an image that portrayed a Hollywood feeling.

I searched through some portraits I had done a while back, remembering one particular photo that had a '40s black and white movie feeling to it. I scanned in the photo, using a resolution of 100 dpi (see fig. 6.39). A higher resolution was not needed, as this image was intended for online viewing.

If you don't have any suitable photographs in your own collection, you can find some quite easily. They are available on the web (use a search engine to find them), from stock photo agencies (although this can be expensive), and on CD-ROM. Many of the CD-ROM versions have pretty good licensing agreements, especially if the intended use is for personal or nonprofit web site use.

Figure 6.38

Torn paper edge border.

Figure 6.39

Marianne.

This portrait had been printed full-frame, a process that left a fairly large border along the sides and kept the 35 mm film proportions.

This really helped in achieving the look I was after. Of course, the image could have been cropped or rotated in Paint Shop Pro. In fact, I resampled the image so the width-to-height ratio would leave the height with a dimension that was a multiple of 10. This made it easy to add the sprocket holes and still have the image match up when tiled vertically.

Leave 4 pixels of space (white in the case of this image), followed by 6 pixels of black to represent the hole. Make the sprocket holes 10 pixels wide.

Use the Brush tool to draw the first couple of holes (squares), as in figure 6.40. You might want to zoom in to about 5:1 to simplify the placement and drawing of the holes.

After you have drawn a few of the holes, you can easily copy and paste the rest down the left side of the photo. It is then a simple matter to copy and paste the whole line of holes from the left side of the photo to the right. The result should resemble figure 6.41.

Figure 6.40

Adding sprocket holes.

Figure 6.41

Final image.

All that's left is to turn this image into an edge border. First, resample the image so it's a more appropriate size for the web. I resampled this image down to 75×92. (If you need to review *resampling*, see the "Resizing and Resampling" section in Chapter 3, "Graphics Quality.")

Open a new file that's 1200×92 (92 because this is the height of the movie film image). Copy and paste the photo image into the far left side of the edge border image.

With the addition of an appropriate title or logo, the border adds to the overall feeling of a web page without interfering with the textual information presented (see fig. 6.42).

Using Cheats (Built-In Texture Tools)

If you can't find, or don't want to use, any of the prefabricated textures you find on the web, don't worry. Paint Shop Pro 4.0 has a set of built-in texture tools you can use to create an unlimited number of patterns. For example, one of the options available with the Brush tool selected is Paper Texture.

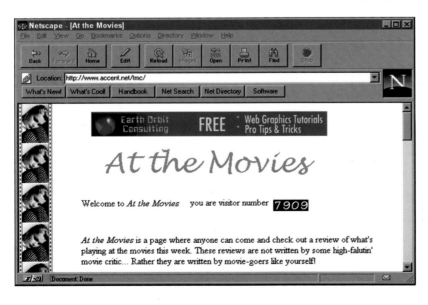

Figure 6.42

At the Movies home page.

Under this option you'll find quite a number of interesting textures. How you use them in combination with some of the features and filters of Paint Shop Pro is what makes them so useful.

To create the texture in figure 6.43, which can easily be made into a background tile, I used an assortment of various pale colors. I also varied the brush size and the paper texture setting as I painted.

After I had a nice layer of colors and textures, I set the foreground color to white and applied a hot wax coating to give the image some dimension.

Applying a darker color of hot wax would change the look of this texture completely. Try it—experiment, experiment!

To create a quick edge border that conveys the feeling of a crumbling brick wall, I started the following figure with a reddish color and a medium brick paper texture. After sketching in the left side of the image, I switched the paper texture to Asphalt. I then filled in the middle and the right side of the image using a pale yellow-green color. To give this image some dimension, I once again applied a hot wax coating, using white as the foreground color (see fig. 6.44).

Figure 6.43

Colorful tile created with Paint Shop Pro.

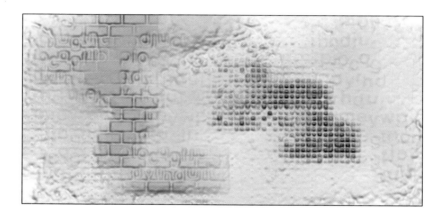

Figure 6.44

Broken brick wall pattern.

Figure 6.44 would be a good candidate for an edge border after making it a seamless tile.

Both figures (6.43 and 6.44) were created in a matter of minutes, with little planning and just an idea for a textured image.

If these textures are a little too wild for you and you'd like something more realistic or natural, try the following to yield a fairly natural wood texture.

Open a new 400×200×16.7 million color file. Set the foreground color to a rich brown. I used R:115 G:41 B:9.

Choose the Fill tool with the fill style set to Solid Color. Then click anywhere in the image to fill it with the brown color.

Set the foreground color to a reddish brown or wine color. I used R:189 G:3 B:51.

Choose the Brush tool with the brush type set to normal, the size set to 150, the shape set to square, and the paper texture set to wood grain.

Sweeping the tool over the image with a couple of strokes should yield something like figure 6.45.

Wow! Pretty cool, and all that in a couple of minutes work.

Set the foreground color to white and, this time, apply two coatings of hot wax. The result should resemble figure 6.46.

Figure 6.45

Reddish wood grain created with Paint Shop Pro.

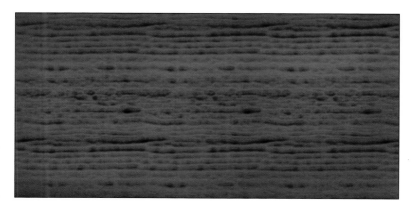

Figure 6.46

Reddish wood grain with added dimension.

To achieve a distinctive aged-wood look, start by filling the image with a pinkish-beige color (I used R:244 G:215 B:198). Sweep the image with the wood grain pattern as above, using the reddish brown color (R:189 G:3 B:51).

Set the foreground color back to the pinkish-beige color and apply a hot wax coating. The result should resemble figure 6.47.

Looks like a piece of wood torn from a run-down barn, doesn't it?

To try a variation that looks like "aged" wood, choose Colors, Colorize and set the Hue to 20 and the Saturation to 50. To achieve an even more weathered look, choose Colors, Adjust,

Brightness/Contrast and set the Brightness to 25 and the Contrast to 0. This will leave you with figure 6.48.

Summary

You can start to get the feeling now of how truly unlimited the possibilities are. I encourage you to take the time to sit down and experiment with Paint Shop Pro. Although these last few images were all created in a matter of minutes, I have at times spent hours playing with the program and have discarded many designs or ideas that didn't quite work out. But no matter; all that time spent is worth it when the result is a graphic that's really original.

Figure 6.47

"Aged" reddish wood grain.

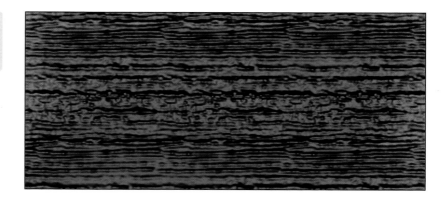

Figure 6.48

"Aged" or "weathered" wood grain texture.

The next section of the book will deal with *filters*. Some of the filters you can use to create special effects are part of Paint Shop Pro. Others can be purchased separately from third-party vendors such as Alien Skin Software, and still others can be found as freeware or shareware if you search the web.

Chapter 7

Filters

This chapter will cover the use of both built-in and third-party filters. Built-in filters are those that come with Paint Shop Pro, and third-party filters are written by other software companies. I'll take a look at all the built-in filters, as well as the filters from Alien Skin Software I use for my graphic work. There are many additional filters available that I don't mention here, but they are commonly discussed on the graphics newsgroups on Usenet. For a list of some of the newsgroups I frequent, see the Resources section at the back of this book.

The following topics will be covered:

- ▶ Using Filters
- ▶ Paint Shop Pro's Built-in Filters
    - ▶ The Drop Shadow Filters
    - ▶ The Cut-Out Filters
    - ▶ The Hot Wax Filters
    - ▶ Seamless Tiles (The Easy Way)
    - ▶ Buttonizing
    - ▶ Creating Textured Buttons with the Buttonize Filter
- ▶ Third-Party Filters
- ▶ Installing and Using Third-Party Filters

- ▶ Black Box Filters by Alien Skin Software
  - ▶ The Carve Filter
  - ▶ The Cut-Out Filter
  - ▶ The Drop Shadow Filter
  - ▶ The Glass Filter
  - ▶ The Glow Filter
  - ▶ The Hue, Saturation, and Brightness (HSB) Noise Filter
  - ▶ Using the Inner Bevel Filter for Metallic Effects
  - ▶ Using the Inner Bevel Filter for Plastic Effects
  - ▶ The Outer Bevel Filter
  - ▶ The Motion Trail Filter
  - ▶ The Swirl Filter
  - ▶ Combining Filters for Special Effects

Using Filters

Most good paint programs these days are *extensible*; that is, they have the capability to run add-on programs. In paint programs such as Photoshop or Paint Shop Pro, these add-ons are known as *plug-ins* or *filters*.

These filters can add a lot of functionality to the paint program, making some tasks easier or even enabling the designer to create certain effects that would be nearly impossible without their use.

For example, adding an inner bevel to text can be accomplished quickly and easily with Alien Skin's Inner Bevel filter. I demonstrated one way to create this look in Chapter 5, "Getting Your Message Across." The Inner Bevel filter, though, has a lot more flexibility and options than discussed there. Other filters, such as the built-in Chisel filter, create a look that would be impossible to do otherwise.

The variety and number of plug-ins available is impressive. Some of these plug-ins come with the programs. Others can be purchased from third-party software companies, and still others are available for free or as shareware on the web.

In this chapter, I will discuss the built-in filters that come with Paint Shop Pro 4.0, as well as the Black Box filters from Alien Skin. In the final section of this chapter, I'll demonstrate the new Eye Candy filters from Alien Skin.

Paint Shop Pro's Built-in Filters

New with Paint Shop Pro 4.0 are a couple of nice built-in filters. You've seen some of these used already in the previous tutorials. For the most part, the included filters are meant to increase Paint Shop Pro's functionality as a web graphics program.

All of these filters deserve some exploration. By playing around and letting your imagination take over, you'll be truly surprised by what you can accomplish—easy but unique drop shadows, great-looking cut-outs, chrome text, simple seamless tiles, and amazing-looking buttons created from any image you can imagine.

The Drop Shadow Filter

The Drop Shadow filter (Image, Special Effects, Add Drop Shadow) adds a drop shadow to a selection such as text. Because different colors can be used and because negative values can be used for the horizontal and vertical offsets, a variety of effects can be created. An example of one of these effects is shown in figure 7.1.

This is, of course, figure 6.45, the wood grain texture from Chapter 6, "Backgrounds and Borders," with some raised text. The raised text has the same texture as the background, though. This effect was achieved by using the Fill tool and the Drop Shadow filter.

To add raised text with the Drop Shadow filter, first open a texture file.

Choose the Text tool and type some text.

With the text still selected, choose the Fill tool and set the Fill style to Pattern. Click on the Options box and, under New Pattern Source, select the current texture image. Click on OK.

Click anywhere within the selected text to fill it with the texture.

Because the text is still selected, you should be able to move it around by switching back to any of the Selection tools. Move the text just a little so the pattern doesn't match up exactly with the background. This will add a "professional" touch to the illusion.

Choose Image, Special Effects, Add Drop Shadow.

Set the Color to black, the Opacity to 150, the Blur to 0, and both the Vertical and Horizontal Offsets to 2. Click on OK. This will create a shadow on the textured text.

Now repeat the process, but switch the color to white and set the offsets to −2. This will add a highlight to the textured text.

Because of adding a drop shadow in both directions and using both a shadow color and a highlight color, the text looks as though it was created by carving away the wood material from around the letters.

By simply reversing the highlight and shadow, you can make the text appear to be carved *into* the background, as in figure 7.2.

Figure 7.1

Raised, textured text created with Drop Shadow filter.

Figure 7.2

Carved, textured text created with Drop Shadow filter.

Both of these illusions assume the light is coming in from the top left. This seems to be the norm for lighting, probably because of the right-hand–centric world we live in.

Naturally, the drop shadow effect can be used to just add plain drop shadows to text or any other selected object.

Play around with the opacity, blur, and offsets to see how these settings affect the shadow look.

Figures 7.3 and 7.4 had the same Add Drop Shadow filter applied.

Figure 7.3 has a darker, harsher shadow and figure 7.4 has a lighter, softer one. The shadow

in figure 7.4 is also offset a little farther out than that in figure 7.3.

These two different looks were achieved by changing the various settings in the Drop Shadow filter. The harsher shadow in figure 7.3 results from a higher opacity and lower blur setting. The softer shadow in figure 7.4 comes from a higher blur and lower opacity.

Another variable to consider with the drop shadow effect is color choice. Paint Shop Pro enables you to choose from a couple of colors for the shadow. Better yet, it also allows you to choose either the current foreground or background color. Figure 7.5 uses a lighter shade of the text color as the shadow color, creating another unique look.

Figure 7.3

Text with harsh shadow.

Figure 7.4

Text with soft shadow.

SHADOW

Figure 7.5

Red text with similar color drop shadow.

The Cut-Out Filter

The Cut-Out filter, though not often used, can help add a three-dimensional effect to your images. This filter is kind of an inside drop shadow, giving the illusion that the object has been cut out of its surroundings. Look at figure 7.6 to see what I mean (you saw this button in Chapter 4, "Essential Elements of Your Web Page"). The text seems to have been cut out of the button. The appearance of the shadow inside the text, along with the shadow from the button itself, adds to the illusion that the button is floating above the page.

Because the Cut-Out filter allows you to select the fill color from the current foreground or background color, you can create the illusion that the text is stamped into the background, as shown in figure 7.7.

To create this image, simply start out with a new 500×200×16.7 million color file and fill it with a color. Swap the foreground and background colors by clicking on the bent two-headed arrow to the lower left of the foreground/background color swatch.

Choose the Text tool and add some text to the image.

Figure 7.6

A button with cut-out text.

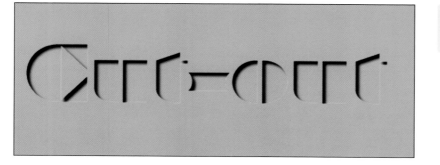

Figure 7.7

Cut-out text.

With the text still selected, choose Image, Special Effects, Cutout. Select Fill Interior With Color. Set the Interior Color to Background Color and select Black as the Shadow Color. Set the Opacity to 255, the Blur to 9, and both Vertical and Horizontal Offsets to 4.

The Hot Wax Filter

I think this filter alone is worth the price you pay for Paint Shop Pro. I haven't seen a comparable filter anywhere. For example, you've seen how the Hot Wax filter can add dimension to text and how it can help give a gold appearance to text (in Chapter 5). You've even seen it create a weathered wood grain look in Chapter 6. In all the previous examples of this filter, it was used in conjunction with other effects. This time you'll achieve a certain effect with this filter alone.

Start with a 500×200×16.7 million color image.

Leave the background color set to white when you create this image.

Set the foreground color to white.

Choose the Text tool and type some text with a large, bold font. I used Braggadocio set at 72 points, with Bold selected. With the background and text both in white, all you'll see is the marquee in the shape of your text, as shown in figure 7.8. (Don't worry if the marquee doesn't seem to be there—Paint Shop Pro suspends display of the marquee while you move it, so it disappears until you let the button up to see where you are.)

Choose Selections, Modify, Feather and set the Feather value to 8 in the Feather Selection dialog box. Click on OK.

This will enlarge the selection so it resembles figure 7.9.

Now the fun begins!

Choose Image, Special Effects, Hot Wax Coating, and reapply the hot wax.

After three coatings, you will start to see some changes in your image (see fig. 7.10).

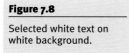

Figure 7.8

Selected white text on white background.

Still nothing spectacular, right?

Apply the hot wax four more times, though, and you'll be surprised! After seven applications of white wax on white text on a white background, you get the result shown in figure 7.11.

Voilà! *Chrome text!* This is an example of the kind of image you can come up with by rolling up your sleeves and playing around with the program. If you didn't see this one with your own eyes, you probably wouldn't believe it. In fact you might have to sit down and try this one before you do believe it.

Why this works is a mystery, but who cares when it's such a great look? This effect is a good example of why I encourage you to experiment, experiment, experiment.

Seamless Tiles (The Easy Way)

Paint Shop Pro 4.0 also has a built-in feature that really helps in the creation of seamless tiles. This option has a couple of drawbacks, though. For one, when you use this feature you must leave a fairly large margin around the selected area (how large depends on the figure). Another small drawback is that this built-in filter tends to soften the edges of your

selection. With some images, this effect is not too noticeable. Some images will need a little retouching, though, and with others you might want to revert to the method outlined at the beginning of Chapter 6.

I'd recommend you give the built-in method a try first, as it can be a major time (and headache) saver.

I'll show you a few samples here to give you an idea of the strengths and weaknesses of this feature.

Open an image you'd like to make a background tile from. I'll use the image in figure 7.12.

Choose the Selection tool, with the Selection Type set to Rectangle and Feather set to 0.

Make a selection, being sure to leave plenty of room between the edges of your selection and the edges of the image. Choose Image, Special

Effects, Create Seamless Pattern. You might get a warning window that says: **Your selection is too close to the edge of the image to complete this operation. Please move your selection farther away from the image's edge**.

In this case, you must re-do the selection and, as it says, move farther away from the edges. This might, unfortunately, leave you with a smaller selection and therefore a smaller image which, when tiled, will form too noticeable a pattern. If this happens, switch to the tried-and-true method discussed at the beginning of Chapter 6, or else find a larger image from which to cut a selection.

After you've created a tile, test out how it will look by creating a larger image and filling it with the tile pattern.

Figure 7.13 shows the tile I created from the texture in figure 7.12.

Figure 7.12

Wild pattern created with different paper textures, colors, and Hot Wax.

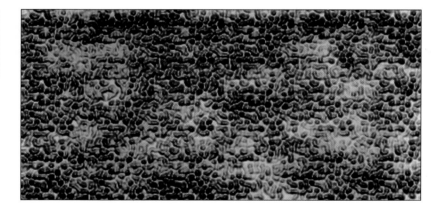

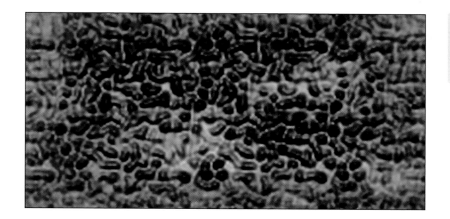

Figure 7.13

Seamless tile created
from figure 7.12 with
Seamless Tile filter.

You might already notice from looking at this figure how Paint Shop Pro has softened the edges a little. To see the effect this will have on your web page's background, open a new file several times larger than the tile.

Choose the Fill tool and set the Fill Style to Pattern. Click on the Options button.

In the Define New Pattern dialog box under New Pattern Source, select the filename of the tile. Then click on OK.

Left-click anywhere in the new graphic to fill it with the tile pattern. As you can see in figure 7.14, the softening has had an obvious effect on this tile; consequently, this image would not be a good choice to use in combination with the built-in Seamless Tile filter.

On the other hand, the following scan of crumpled computer paper might work out a little better (see fig. 7.15). The lower contrast and softer underlying pattern of this image is better suited to tiling with the built-in filter.

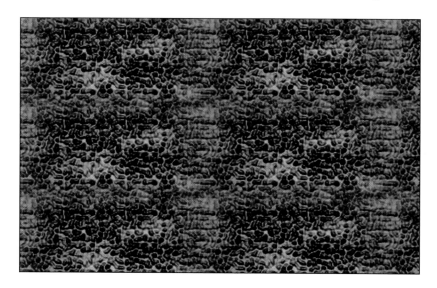

Figure 7.14

Image filled with seamless tile.

Figure 7.15

Scan of crumpled computer paper.

Figure 7.16 is the result of making a selection and running the Seamless Tile filter.

Figure 7.16

Seamless tile created with Seamless Tile filter.

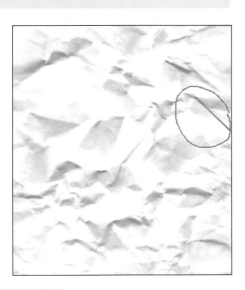

The only obvious problem is the dark line near the top right corner (highlighted in red). Use the Eyedropper tool and the Brush tool, followed by the Retouch tool, to get rid of the line. You should end up with something like figure 7.17.

Figure 7.17

Finished seamless tile.

Tiling the image in figure 7.17 produces a perfect seamless background, as in figure 7.18. It's almost impossible to tell where the seams are. It's also very difficult to see the repeating pattern, and the retouching involved was minimal.

From this you can see that, with the right pattern, the built-in filter is very easy to use. The idea is to come up with a pattern that will work *with* the limitations instead of against them, and you might have to try a few before you find a good one. Again, of course, you can use the tried-and-true method outlined in Chapter 6 if the built-in filter doesn't yield acceptable results.

Figure 7.18

Image filled with seamless tile.

Buttonizing

This addition to Paint Shop Pro 4.0, the Buttonize filter, was a big selling point when this latest version of the program was introduced.

A couple of mouse clicks can turn any image into a button. Although the Buttonize filter is rather limited, you can come up with some fairly neat effects in minutes and without much work at all.

By cropping and resampling one of my portrait photos, I created the button shown in figure 7.19.

After cropping and resampling the photo you have selected to work with, choose Image, Special Effects, Buttonize. Set the Edge Size (%) to 5 and select Transparent Edge.

Figure 7.19

"Buttonized" photo of Marianne.

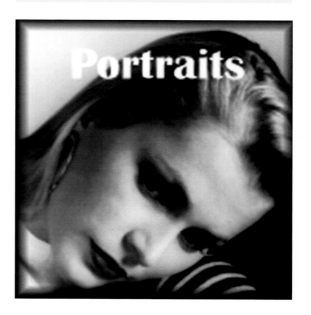

The Current Background color in the background color swatch plays a role in the final look of the button. The next four figures (7.20–7.23) were all created by filling a rectangle with a light blue color.

Each image then had the Buttonize filter applied. The difference is that the background color was changed for each button. The background colors used were red, white, the same light blue as the foreground, and a dark blue.

Figure 7.20

Figure 7.21

Figure 7.22

Figure 7.23

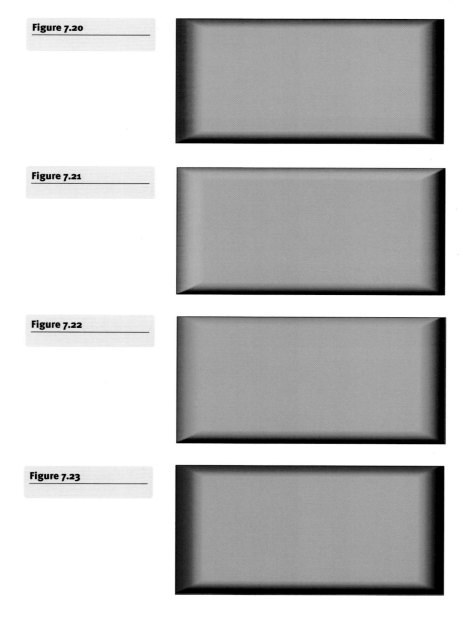

Creating Textured Buttons with the Buttonize Filter

Another quick button can be created by cutting a suitable size rectangle from, for example, the wood grain texture created in Chapter 6.

After you've cropped out the size you want, set the Background Color to one of the colors in the wood grain itself, and then choose Image, Special Effects, Buttonize.

Set the Edge Size (%) to 10 and select Transparent Edge.

This will create a button similar to the one in figure 7.24.

Quite an attractive button for so little work! Before the Buttonize filter was available, you'd have to play around with masks and spend a lot of time to create such a textured button.

Now you can save this button, colorize it, and apply text as needed, and have a ton of buttons available in a matter of minutes.

That accounts for all the Paint Shop Pro filters. The next sections will discuss some of the many third-party filters available.

■ Note

Visit Alien Skin (some of the nicest folks I've done business with, bar none!) at
`http://www.alienskin.com`.

Metatools has a site at
`http://www.metatools.com`.

Digital Showbiz LTD has a site with a collection of filters that is hard to describe—you'd have to see them for yourself.
`http://www.dsb.com/products/dsbflux.html`

And there are tons more out there!

Third-Party Filters

Third-party refers to a software company other than the company that produced the main program. Many companies produce plug-in filters for Photoshop-compatible programs such as Paint Shop Pro, including Alien Skin Software (Black Box and Eye Candy) and Metatools (Kai's Power Tools). Naturally, companies such as these usually have web sites and sometimes offer free demo versions of their filters.

The plug-in filters these companies produce add tons of functionality to a paint program,

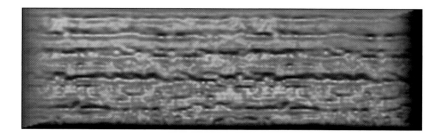

Figure 7.24

Wood-grain–textured button created with the Buttonize filter.

enabling the artist to quickly create the special effects described in this chapter.

Installing and Using Third-Party Filters

To install third-party filters for use with Paint Shop Pro, simply follow the setup instructions that come with the filters. Then, in Paint Shop Pro, under File, Preferences, General Program Preferences, click the Plug-In Filters tab. Make sure Enable Plug-in Filters is selected and that the directory where you've installed the filters is correct. After re-starting Paint Shop Pro, you should see the new filters available under Image, Plug-In Filters.

Black Box Filters by Alien Skin Software

Of all the third-party plug-ins I've used, the Black Box (and its latest incarnation, Eye Candy) filters are my personal favorites. In the remainder of this chapter on filters, I am going

to devote some space to a demonstration of what can be achieved with Alien Skin's products, because I want to emphasize the benefits of a really good add-on. I suggest you drop by Alien Skin's web site and pick up their latest set of demo filters.

The collection of ten filters in the Black Box are not only functional—they are also extremely fun to play with.

Black Box comes with a great interface that displays a real-time preview of the effect. This helps you decide the exact setting for the effect before you commit to it.

Figure 7.25 shows the preview window for the Drop Shadow plug-in.

At the left is the real-time preview window. The gray window in the middle displays the current settings, which can be changed by sliding the red balls. As you move the red sliders, the preview window updates so you can see exactly what effect the settings will have on your image.

Figure 7.25

Alien Skin's Black Box.

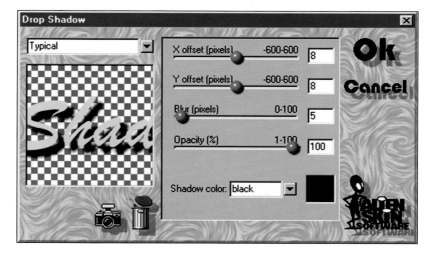

Another nice feature is the extensive set of default values built into each of the ten filters. Above the preview window in figure 7.25, you can see a pull-down menu that currently shows the word "Typical." On this menu are preset values you can use or modify.

The Carve Filter

The Carve filter creates the opposite effect of the Inner Bevel filter. Where the Inner Bevel makes an object seem to lift out of the image, the Carve filter makes the image appear to be carved into the surface of the image. This is a little hard to visualize, but if you imagine the light coming in from the upper left in figure 7.26, you can see how the text appears to sink into the image.

By contrast, figure 7.27 was created with a similar setting but with the Inner Bevel filter.

It might still be a little difficult to see the difference. Both effects are based on a similar optical illusion, so don't worry if you can't see much of a difference.

The Cut-Out Filter

The Cut-Out filter produces a similar effect to the one included with Paint Shop Pro 4.0. One nice function Alien Skin adds, of course, is the real-time preview.

The Drop Shadow Filter

Again, this filter offers some built-in settings and the preview. In addition, the offset values of this filter have a very large range, going from –600 to 600 pixels in both the horizontal and vertical directions.

Figure 7.26

Carved text created with Alien Skin's Black Box.

Figure 7.27

Inner Beveled text created with Alien Skin's Black Box.

The Glass Filter

With only the text selected, the Glass filter produces an image like the one in figure 7.28.

You can see how it resembles the Inner Bevel or Carve filter; however, when the text is deselected and the Glass filter is applied to the entire image, something completely different is created (see fig. 7.29).

It looks as though the letters are at the bottom of the deep end of a swimming pool. Nifty, eh?

This effect is so cool I have actually thought about creating a web site around this image.

The Glow Filter

The Glow filter reproduces the neon effect described in Chapter 5 (see fig. 7.30). Of course, Alien Skin's Black Box enables you to create wider splashes or glows than the method outlined in Chapter 5, which talks about text.

Figure 7.28

Text with Alien Skin's Glass filter applied.

Figure 7.29

Entire image with Glass filter applied.

Figure 7.30

Text with Glow filter applied.

The Hue, Saturation, and Brightness (HSB) Noise Filter

The HSB Noise filter might, at first glance, seem to be of limited use. By applying this filter in conjunction with other effects, though, you can obtain some interesting patterns that make playing around worthwhile. For example, I'll show you how to create a burlap texture.

Open a new 400×200×16.7 million color image.

Set the foreground color to white and add some text.

Note

The B in HSB stands for *brightness*. Some programs use HSL instead of HSB. Paint Shop Pro uses HSL, where the L stands for *luminance*. Luminance and brightness are equivalent.

Apply the HSB Noise filter with the preset More Hue Protected Noise selected (see fig. 7.31).

Choose Image, Normal Filters, Blur More to obtain the results in figure 7.32.

Figure 7.31

Noise filter applied to text selection.

Figure 7.32

Blur More filter applied.

Now run the Edge Enhance More filter by choosing Image, Edge Filters, Edge Enhance More. This will give you a nice burlap texture, as in figure 7.33.

Running the Edge Enhance More filter a couple more times yields the interesting variation seen in figure 7.34. Looks something like the static you see on a television that's not picking up a clear signal, right?

Using the Inner Bevel Filter for Metallic Effects

In my opinion, the Inner Bevel filter is the real workhorse of this set of filters. The coolest web page buttons are easy to create with the help of this filter, as are metallic- or plastic-looking text.

To see the power of this filter, open a new 200×100×16.7 million color file.

Choose the Selection tool, with the Selection Type set to Rectangle and the Feather option set to 0. Draw a rectangular selection.

Set the Selection Type to Circle.

Position the cursor along the top left of the selection about as far from the left side of the rectangle selection as half the height of the rectangle.

Hold down the shift key and make a circular selection to the left of the rectangle. Repeating this process on the right should give you a round-end rectangular selection, as shown in figure 7.35.

Figure 7.33

Text with burlap texture.

Figure 7.34

Text with "static" pattern.

Figure 7.35

Shape created with multiple selections.

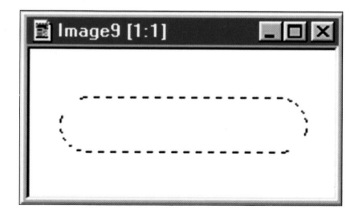

Filters

Note

Using the Selection tools in this manner is somewhat challenging, but with a little practice it becomes easier. I know from experience, believe me. I'll cover this method in more detail in the section on "Drawing With Selections" in Chapter 8, "Special Techniques."

Fill the selection with a metallic gold (see fig. 7.36). I used a favorite gold fill I created in another program, but you can use the one that was used for the gold text or some other fill.

Figure 7.36

Shape filled with gold gradient.

Choose Image, Plug-In Filters, Alien Skin, Inner Bevel and use the preset "button." This will look like figure 7.37.

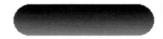

Figure 7.37

Inner Bevel filter applied.

Whoa! Pretty cool already.

Choose the Selection tool and make a circular selection near the right side of the button.

Set the foreground color to red.

Choose the Fill tool and set the Tolerance to 200.

Click anywhere within the selection to fill it with red (see fig. 7.38).

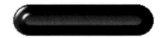

Figure 7.38

Red light added.

With the circle still selected, run the Inner Bevel filter again with the same setting. This will yield a nice three-dimensional button, complete except for text, as in figure 7.39.

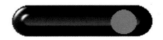

Figure 7.39

3D effect added to red light by using Inner Bevel filter.

I used buttons similar to this on the GrafX Design site, using red and green to give visual clues to viewers, as a guide to which page they are on. All the buttons with a green "light" take them to another page, while a red "light" signifies the current page.

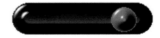

The Inner Bevel filter can help with text effects, as well. The gold text in figure 7.40 was created by filling some text with a gold gradient pattern and applying the Inner Bevel filter.

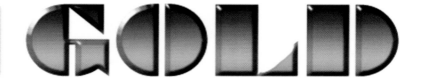

Figure 7.40

Gold text created with
gold gradient and Inner
Bevel filter.

Instead of using one of the presets this time, I tried the following settings:

Bevel Width: 5

Shadow Depth: 33

Smoothness: 4

Drop Off: Flat

Highlight Brightness: 100

Highlight Sharpness: 32

Lighting: Direction 135 and Angle 45

Using the Inner Bevel Filter for Plastic Effects

In addition to a metallic look, you can achieve a plastic look for text by using the Inner Bevel

filter. Using the "button" preset gave the text in figure 7.41 a shiny, plastic finish.

Figure 7.41 was created by adding light blue text to a light blue background and running the Inner Bevel filter on it. The addition of a drop shadow, in tight and with very little blurring, added to the illusion.

Looks kind of like the text you'd get from one of those label guns and the small strips of plastic, doesn't it?

This is definitely a filter worth some exploration time!

The Outer Bevel Filter

The Outer Bevel yields the opposite look from that of the Inner Bevel filter, making text or any other selection appear to rise up from the rest of the image. The image in figure 7.42 was created by using the Slightly Raised option.

Figure 7.41

Plastic text created with
Inner Bevel filter.

Figure 7.42

Text with Outer Bevel
filter applied.

The Motion Trail Filter

The Motion Trail filter, as its name implies, adds a motion trail to a selected area of your image. To demonstrate this plug-in, I created a quick sketch of a cyclist (see fig. 7.43).

First I made a couple of selections on the sketch by using the Lasso tool, as seen in figure 7.44.

Then I applied the Motion Trail filter. I used the default Typical setting, changing only the direction of the trail to 180 degrees and deselecting the Edges Only option. The result can be seen in figure 7.45. The static sketch of the cyclist now has a dynamic movement quality.

Figure 7.43

Original Cyclist sketch.

Figure 7.44

Portions of sketch selected with Lasso tool.

Figure 7.45

Motion filter applied to Cyclist sketch.

The Swirl Filter

The Swirl filter can be used to create really neat patterns for backgrounds or buttons.

Start with a new 200×200×16.7 million color image.

Select a foreground color and use the Brush tool to draw some lines. Change colors and brush sizes if you wish.

After you have an image resembling figure 7.46, run the Alien Skin Swirl filter on it. This will leave you with a pattern suitable for tiling or creating buttons (see fig. 7.47).

Figure 7.46

Random color lines.

Figure 7.47

Swirl filter applied to random colored lines.

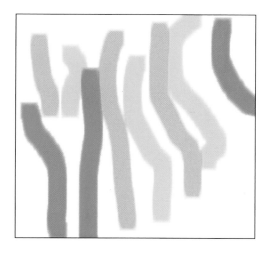

Combining Filters for Special Effects: Alien Skin's Eye Candy

Running multiple filters on a selection can yield some wild results. In fact, some of the text effects shown in Chapter 5 were the result of using masks and a combination of blurring, brightening, and such.

In this section I'll introduce you to the new Eye Candy filters from Alien Skin and use a couple of them to demonstrate what you can accomplish by using multiple filters.

Eye Candy 3.0 from Alien Skin Software is the latest incarnation of their Black Box filters. In addition to sporting a new interface (see fig. 7.48) and containing the 10 filters from the Black Box, Eye Candy has the following 11 filters (we'll discuss several of them in this section).

▶ Anti-Matter

▶ Chrome

▶ Fur

▶ Star

▶ Smoke

▶ Squint

▶ Jiggle

▶ Water Drops

▶ Weave

▶ Fire

▶ Perspective Shadow

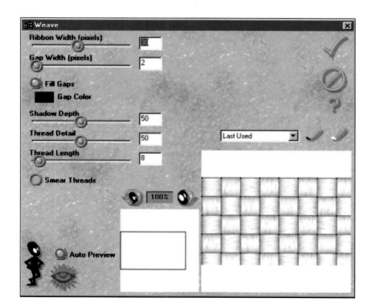

Figure 7.48

Alien Skin Software's Eye Candy 3.0.

The next examples will showcase some of the new Eye Candy filters and demonstrate what is possible by applying multiple filters. I'll take some ordinary text and make it appear as though it's actually melting, flaming, smoking metal text.

Start with a new 600×250×16.7 million color image with a white background.

Set the foreground color to white and type some text.

Choose Image, Plug-In Filters, Eye Candy 3.0, Chrome. Then either choose one of the defaults or play around until you see something you like in the real-time preview window. When you get a result you like, click on the check mark to apply it.

I chose the chrome look shown in figure 7.49.

Apply the Perspective Shadow filter, setting the shadow so it displays back and to the left, as in figure 7.50.

Continue by running the Eye Candy Smoke filter, adjusting the smoke so it doesn't run off the top of the image. The result should resemble figure 7.51.

Figure 7.49

Text with Eye Candy's Chrome filter applied.

Figure 7.50

Perspective shadow added.

Figure 7.51

Smoke filter applied.

Add a little flame with Image, Plug-In Filters, Eye Candy 3.0, Fire, again making sure the flames don't run off the top (see fig. 7.52).

Finally, run the Eye Candy Jiggle filter to give the illusion that the text is warping and buckling from the heat, as in figure 7.53.

You'll have to be careful with the settings so the text remains readable. If you "Jiggle" the text too much, it'll still resemble something that's on fire, but what exactly is burning will be anybody's guess.

Figure 7.53 demonstrates one example of what can be achieved with the use of multiple filters, whether built-ins or plug-ins.

Summary

Again, I highly encourage you to play around with whatever graphics tools you have and see what you can come up with. The only limit is your own imagination (and your budget)!

If your only concern is creating your own home pages, the built-in filters along with some of the other techniques used in this book should be enough to get you started. If, on the other hand, you're competing with other web designers or just want to add something a little more professional to your arsenal of graphics tools, you might want to consider the added expense of third-party filters.

Figure 7.52

Flame added.

Figure 7.53

Jiggle filter applied to give illusion of melting.

Chapter 8

Special Techniques

I f you've been going through the book chapter by chapter, you're getting familiar with Paint Shop Pro and some of the things you can do with it. Now that you're comfortable, I'm going to throw some surprises at you.

This chapter will show you a couple of neat tricks you never would have imagined you could pull off with Paint Shop Pro, from transparent GIFs and imagemaps to masks and colorizing black and white photographs. And, even if you never thought you could draw, I'll show you how to turn a photograph into a pencil sketch. All of this and more, using only the options and filters that ship with Paint Shop Pro.

By this point you've probably gone through at least some of the other techniques, so I might be a little more brief in my explanations here. If you find yourself scratching your head in dismay, try backing up a few steps and making sure the image you're working on is similar to the one presented in the book. As always, I'll try to be as clear as possible.

- ▶ Transparent GIFs
  - ▶ Creating Transparent GIFs
- ▶ Imagemaps
  - ▶ Adding Imagemaps to Your Web Site: Understanding the Code
  - ▶ Locating Imagemap Coordinates
  - ▶ Imagemaps Versus Buttons
  - ▶ Button Bars as Imagemaps
  - ▶ Beyond Button Bars—Getting Fancy

- ▶ The Magic of Masks
    - ▶ Beveled Buttons
- ▶ Making Selections for Special Effects
- ▶ Drawing with Selections
- ▶ Photo Special Effects
    - ▶ Colorizing Black and White Photos
    - ▶ Photo Aging and Vignettes
    - ▶ Converting Photos into Drawings

Transparent GIFs

A day never goes by that I don't see someone on the Internet asking how they can make part of an image transparent. They ask the question in different ways—sometimes they don't know exactly how to phrase the question—but it is being asked.

Here's one thing to keep in mind: For now, the only way you can have any portion of an image appear transparent is for that image to be a GIF. In fact, the image must be in GIF89a format. The image cannot, and probably never will be, a JPG. We can hope that sometime in the near future browsers will support the PNG format, which also allows transparent pixels. Until that time arrives, however, to be transparent, an image will have to be a GIF.

If you've never heard of transparent GIFs, you might be asking yourself what makes them important enough for people to ask about them every day.

One of the main reasons you would want some portion of an image to be transparent is to eliminate having a border when an irregularly shaped image with feathered, blurred, or shadowed edges is displayed on a textured background. In other words, say you have a background tile on your web pages, and you want to display a title logo. Now, say the logo has an irregular shape—it's not rectangular. If you place the logo on the pages over the tiled background without using the transparent GIF format, the logo will include an undesirable square or rectangular background left over from the image's creation.

Some people try to get around this background problem by using the background tile for the background of the logo, but this method rarely produces an acceptable result. There really is no way to get the tile background of the logo image to match up with the tiled background, and the end product can look frustratingly amateurish. The only viable option is to create the logo and save it as a GIF, with the transparent option enabled and the background color of the logo set as the transparent color.

Figures 8.1 and 8.2 show the difference between what a logo without a transparent background and the same one with a transparent background would look like on a web page with a textured background.

Creating Transparent GIFs

To create a transparent GIF, first open a copy of the image you'll be placing the GIF against. I'll use the following wood texture image that was created at the end of Chapter 6, "Backgrounds and Borders" (see fig. 8.3).

Figure 8.1

Logo without transparent
background.

Figure 8.2

Logo with transparent
background.

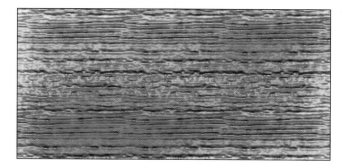

Figure 8.3

Wood grain texture.

The next step is to choose the Eyedropper tool and select a color from the textured image that you feel is fairly predominant. Move the Eyedropper tool over the patterned image and click the left mouse button. This sets the current foreground color to the color the Eyedropper tool is over.

Once you've chosen the color with the Eyedropper, open a new file with the same dimensions. Choose the Fill tool, set the Fill Style to Solid Color and click anywhere in the new image to fill it with the background color you've decided on.

Select a new foreground color and use the Text tool to enter some text, as in figure 8.4 (with Antialias selected, as usual).

Choose Image, Special Effects, Add Drop Shadow to add a drop shadow (see fig. 8.5).

Figure 8.4

Simple text.

Figure 8.5

Drop shadow added.

Because both the text and the drop shadow are antialiased, you should be able to get a good idea of what any image you create and display against the background will look like.

Before you save the final image, use the Eyedropper tool to set the current background color to the color of the background of the image.

Choose the Eyedropper tool and right-click anywhere over the background of the text image.

This action sets the current foreground color (shown in the color swatch) to the color you want to be transparent. If you don't perform this action properly you'll end up with unexpected results.

Choose File, Save As to bring up the Save As dialog box.

Choose GIF—CompuServe from the Save As Type pull-down menu, and choose 89a as the sub-type in the Sub-Type pull-down menu. Whether to choose Interlaced when you save your files is something you'll have to decide for

yourself. For more information about *interlacing*, see the section on "Interlaced GIFs and Progressive JPGs" in Chapter 3, "Graphics Quality."

Click on the Options button to bring up the File Preferences dialog box (see fig. 8.6).

Make sure the third option, Set The Transparency Value to the Background Color, is checked.

The dialog box shown in figure 8.6 offers a preview window showing all the pixels that will be transparent in the GIF file. This feature is useful if you need to check to see if you've used the transparent color where you didn't want it. Also, it shows you if a color you originally

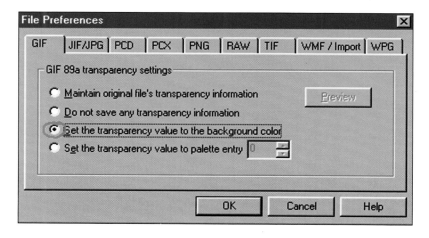

Figure 8.6

File Preferences dialog box.

thought was a single color is now dithered, as can happen when you decrease the color depth to 256 colors. If you have forgotten to decrease the color depth, Paint Shop Pro will remind you to do so before permitting you to save the image as a GIF, but this can prevent the preview from working and cause other problems. If the reminder message box comes up, you really should cancel your Save and decrease the color depth before trying the Save process again.

If you find that the background color has *dithered*, you'll have to fix the problem or your background will not be transparent. This problem can be easily remedied with the Eyedropper and Fill tools, or with the Color Replacer tool. (You might want to review the section on "Dithering Your Graphics" in Chapter 2, "Color Quality.")

Once you're sure you have a solid color background that can be used as the transparent color, save the image as a GIF.

This image can now be displayed against a patterned background tile, as shown in figure 8.7.

If the color match was good, there should be no halo. (Refer to "Choosing the Right Colors" in Chapter 2 for a more in-depth discussion of this topic).

Make note of the color you've chosen so you can create other transparent GIFs to use with the same background tile in the future.

By selecting the same brown color used in figure 8.3 for the background color of the logo in figure 8.8, I was able to easily display the logo over the wood texture background.

Imagemaps

Imagemaps are a great way to add fun and helpful navigability to your web site. They're more interesting than those URL links that seem to bog down your page with unsightly

Figure 8.7

Transparent GIF on a textured background.

Figure 8.8

GrafX Design logo as a transparent GIF.

underlines. And they add a professional quality to your web pages. Imagemaps allow you to create navigational interfaces to your pages.

Adding Imagemaps to Your Web Site: Understanding the Code

Imagemaps are created by using an image in combination with special HTML code. Since I never intended this book to be about HTML but rather about creating web graphics, I didn't want to go into detail about the HTML side of imagemaps. However, you can't get a good feeling for imagemaps without understanding some of the HTML behind them, so I'll have to bend my own rule a little.

The image in figure 8.9 was used for an imagemap on the GrafX Design site (`http://www.grafx-design.com`).

Figure 8.9

GrafX Design imagemap.

The following HTML code (without the line numbers) is used in combination with the image to form an imagemap.

```
1.  <MAP NAME="grafxmap">
2.  <!-- <AREA SHAPE=rect COORDS="134,20,213,48" HREF="index.html"> -->
3.  <AREA SHAPE=rect COORDS="220,20,299,48" HREF="tutorials.html">
4.  <AREA SHAPE=rect COORDS="306,20,385,48" HREF="links.html">
5.  <AREA SHAPE=rect COORDS="392,20,469,48" HREF="about.html">
6.  <AREA SHAPE=rect COORDS="134,53,213,81" HREF="http://www.accent.
    ➥net/tmc/artpage.htm">
7.  <AREA SHAPE=rect COORDS="220,53,299,81" HREF="http://www.accent.
    ➥net/tmc/earth.htm">
8.  <AREA SHAPE=rect COORDS="306,53,385,81" HREF="reviews.html">
9.  <AREA SHAPE=rect COORDS="392,53,469,81" HREF="mailto:webmaster@
    ➥grafx-design.com">
10. </MAP>
11. <img usemap="#grafxmap" border=0 src="newgrafx.jpg" width=512
    ➥height=158>
```

I'll go through the code quickly and explain what each part is for.

Line 1 uses the <MAP> tag to give the map a name. The corresponding </MAP> tag in line 10 closes the map section of the HTML.

Lines 2 through 9 describe areas of the image that are to be mapped. When a viewer moves the mouse over one of these areas, the pointer

■ **Note**

There are many good books available that go into more detail on the subject of imagemaps, as well as other aspects of HTML. The book I started with is Laura Lemay's *Teach Yourself Web Publishing with HTML 3.0* from Sams. Laura Lemay has upgraded this excellent book to take advantage of HTML 3.2.

You can also pick up a few quick tips online, as I did, by pointing your browser at http://www.altavista.com and entering "imagemap" as the search criteria (without the quotes). This will give you a large listing of sites where people have been nice enough to share their expertise.

■ **Note**

I can use the same chunk of HTML for several different pages by commenting out the code that would call the page this code is running. You'll notice that the link to index.html is commented out, meaning I borrowed this code from that page. When I copied and pasted the same HTML into the tutorial page, I commented out the line that calls the tutorials.html page and removed the comments from the index.html line. It isn't necessary to have a link to the current page in a web site, and this can be avoided by commenting out a different line each time the code is used. As a programmer you learn never to rewrite something you've already written and tested, so I cut and paste the code where it's needed.

Special Techniques

changes, indicating a link of some sort. Line 2, though, is *commented out*.

Line 11 is an image tag, with the addition of the *usemap=#image_map*_name option. This line just tells the browser the image is to be used as a map.

You'll notice that each line in the code from 2 through 9 defines an area, the shape of the area, the coordinates of the area, and a link.

Possible shapes include rectangle *(rect)*, circle *(circ)*, and polygons *(poly)*.

Locating Imagemap Coordinates

So far so good, but how exactly can you find out what the coordinates should be? That's where Paint Shop Pro comes in.

If you were to load in the imagemap from figure 8.9 and move the cursor over the image, you would notice the x and y coordinates of the mouse is displayed in real time in the lower left corner of the Paint Shop Pro screen.

If you move the mouse over the upper right corner of the Home button, you'll see that the x and y coordinates equal 134, 20 and the lower right corner of the Home button equals 213, 28. Look familiar? These are the same numbers used to describe the rectangle area in line 2 of the HTML source code. What this all means is that discovering the defined areas is as simple as moving the mouse around your image and jotting down the numbers shown in the lower left corner of the screen.

To describe a circle, you need to find the x and y coordinates of the center and the radius in pixels. This might sound a little complicated, but in reality it's fairly easy. Of course, there are programs out there that will do some, most, or

▮ Note

The imagemaps I'm referring to are called *client-side* imagemaps, because the client computer—the one doing the browsing, as opposed to the host computer or server—runs the necessary code to enable an image to be mapped. Tons more information on both server-side and client-side imagemaps is available in HTML books (such as Laura Lemay's book mentioned previously), as well as on the Internet.

all of this for you, but playing around with an imagemap or two, using the method I've just described, can be a lot quicker than installing and testing out a bunch of new software. I've used Paint Shop Pro so far for all the imagemaps I've done.

Describing a polygonal area is similar to describing a rectangular one, except you pick several points around the perimeter rather than just the upper right and lower left corners.

Imagemaps Versus Buttons

Perhaps you're saying to yourself, "I could just as easily have used a collection of buttons instead of the imagemap shown in figure 8.9." Of course, you'd be right, so I'll explain why I decided to go with the imagemap.

▶ The map combines the GrafX Design logo with the buttons. This allow the logo to be quite small but still visible. It also gives a nice integrated look to the logo and button, similar to a small interface.

▶ When the imagemap is loaded into the browser's cache, it will pop up almost immediately when used on other pages of the same web site.

These are both rather gray areas, though, and you'll have to decide for yourself if your viewers will be better served by a set of buttons or an imagemap. Again, because the web is dynamic, you really should consider changing your pages often. Try out these and many other styles of presenting your information to the people who surf by.

Buttons Bars as Imagemaps

The creation of an attractive button bar as shown in figure 8.10 is a simple matter and can be achieved in only a few minutes.

The shape is created by using the selection method outlined in the Inner Bevel section in Chapter 7, "Filters." It's then filled with the purple color. Dark and light shades of the purple color are used to draw vertical lines to separate the bar into buttons. The inner bevel filter from Alien Skin is applied to give the bar a three-dimensional look and, finally, text is added.

The image is now ready to be used as a button bar.

With the image open in Paint Shop Pro, choose the Selection tool (this enables you to use the

crosshairs of the tool for locating the coordinates of the rectangle shapes used in the HTML code).

Move the cursor over the upper left corner of the button bar. Jot down the coordinates that appear in the lower left of the Paint Shop Pro screen, as seen in figure 8.11.

In figure 8.11, the coordinates show as 2, 2; this is the upper left corner of the first button (Home).

Now, the truth is that the end buttons are not rectangular but have rounded ends. This doesn't matter in the grand scheme of things. When a viewer places the cursor anywhere in the rectangle of the Home button or the E-mail button, a click of the mouse button will lead to the provided link. Whether the viewer clicks in the center of the button or a little outside one of the corners doesn't matter. You could define the circle and then a rectangle for each of the end buttons, but it isn't worth the effort.

Move the mouse to the lower right of the first button and record the x, y coordinates. Continue this way until you have two sets of coordinates for each of the buttons on the button bar.

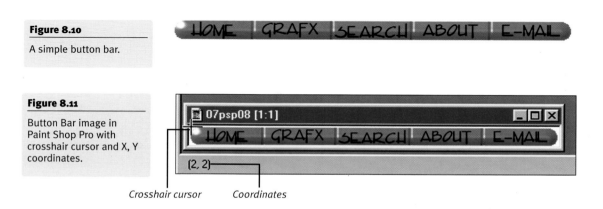

Figure 8.10

A simple button bar.

Figure 8.11

Button Bar image in Paint Shop Pro with crosshair cursor and X, Y coordinates.

Crosshair cursor   Coordinates

Special Techniques

For the image in figure 8.11, I got the following sets of numbers:

- Home (2, 2) (80, 20)
- GrafX (81, 2) (159, 20)
- Search (160, 2) (239, 20)
- About (240, 2) (317, 20)
- E-mail (318, 2) (398, 20)

These coordinates translate into the following HTML imagemap code.

```
1. <MAP NAME="buttonmap">
2. <!-- <AREA SHAPE=rect COORDS="2,2,
   ➥80,20" HREF="home.html"> -->
3. <AREA SHAPE=rect COORDS="81,2,159,20"
   ➥HREF="grafx.html">
4. <AREA SHAPE=rect COORDS="160,2,239,20"
   ➥HREF="search.html">
5. <AREA SHAPE=rect COORDS="240,2,317,20"
   ➥HREF="about.html">
6. <AREA SHAPE=rect COORDS="318,2,398,20"
   ➥HREF="mailto:webmaster@grafx-design.
   ➥com">
7. </MAP>
8. <img usemap="#buttonmap" border=0 src=
   ➥"buttonbar.jpg" width=400 height=22>
```

Line 1 names the map, lines 2–6 define mapped areas, line 7 closes the map tag, and line 8 uses the <IMG> tag to display the imagemap.

Beyond Button Bars— Getting Fancy

You might remember the image in figure 8.12 from Chapter 2.

This metallic copper graphic was an idea for a medieval, cave-and-creatures-type game web site.

It would be hard to implement this image as a set of buttons and retain the fantasy-style appeal. Besides, I like the graphic a lot. So, imagemap to the rescue!

Figure 8.12

Copper imagemap.

Perhaps you're wondering, though, how to map the unusual shapes. Well, the <AREA> tag has a Poly shape option that can be used. To demonstrate how portions of this image could be mapped, I'll zoom in on the Home section and show you one method of dealing with the unusual shape (see fig. 8.13).

By using several x, y pairs to form a polygon, you can get pretty close to defining the circular shape at the edges of each button portion of this image.

Figure 8.13

Close-up of imagemap, showing coordinates.

The same method of describing polygons could be used to highlight states or provinces on an image of a geographical map (thus allowing you to create an imagemap from an image of a map).

The decision to use an imagemap, like many other decisions you'll make as a Webmaster, is not always a clear or easy one to make. Ultimately, the final decision will depend on how well your readers take to your design. If you receive tons of positive e-mail, you'll know you're on the right track.

Although it can take a lot of effort to achieve that nice blend of functionality and fashion, you'll reap the rewards in the form of web site hits.

The Magic of Masks

Masks are one of the most powerful editing tools available to a computer artist. I like to think of them as almost magical, hence the title.

You've seen masks used in some of the text tutorials. I'll take the time here to explain why you'd want to use them and how they do their magic.

The *why* part is the easiest. Masks enable you to perform graphics tricks, such as the "disappearing text" and beveled button described in the following sections, that might be extremely difficult or even impossible otherwise.

The *how* is a little more difficult. A mask is a grayscale image that allows changes to be made to another image. How much change depends on how dark or light the mask is within a certain area. White areas of the mask allow the most change, and black areas permit no change. Areas of gray allow some change—less if the gray is darker and more if the gray is lighter. You might want to think of a mask as a stencil with variable opacity. To understand this better, open a new image and place some text on it as shown in figure 8.14.

<

Blurring

Figure 8.14

Simple text.

Choose Masks, New, Empty. Nothing seems to happen, right? Choose Masks, Edit—your mask will now appear. It will be the same size as the current image but filled completely with black.

Set the foreground color to black and the background color to white.

Choose the Fill tool and set the Fill Style to Linear Gradient.

Click the Options button and set the Direction to 90 degrees in the Gradient Fill Direction dialog box.

Click anywhere in the mask to fill it with the gradient.

To see what your image looks like with the mask in place, choose View, Through Mask. You'll see something like figure 8.15.

The image is still there—it's just masked.

With the mask in place, you can use some filters and effects to see how the mask works. Before you do so, you should toggle off the mask with Masks, Edit.

If there is a check mark next to the word Edit, anything you do will affect the mask itself, just as the linear gradient filled the mask and not the image. Once the mask is complete, though, you want to work on the image *through* the mask. You can also toggle off View, Through Mask, as this has no effect here.

Figure 8.15

Simple text viewed through mask.

Choose Image, Normal Filters, Blur More. The text in the image will now be blurred, but only in degrees, depending on the mask. Because of the black-to-white horizontal fill, the text should not be blurred at all on the left and very blurred on the right, with a linear variation of the blur through the middle of the text as in figure 8.16.

Even after the Blur More filter is applied many times, the left side is hardly affected, while the right side has become very blurred (see fig. 8.17).

Although not all filters or effects work with masks, many can be used in conjunction with a mask or series of masks to create some really cool effects. By using a similar linear gradient fill, for example, you can have text seem to disappear, as in figure 8.18.

After adding text to a new image and creating a mask as outlined above, choose Colors, Adjust, Brightness/Contrast and set %Brightness to 100 and %Contrast to 0. Running this adjustment twice will yield results similar to figure 8.18.

Figure 8.16

Text blurred more to right from application of Blur filter through Linear Gradient mask.

Blurring

Figure 8.17

Blur applied several times through Linear Gradient mask.

Blurring

Figure 8.18

Text fades out with application of Brightness/ Contrast filter through Linear Gradient mask.

Disappearin

Text

Special Techniques

Beveled Buttons

Masks are used to make adjustments to parts of an image without affecting the rest of the image. This comes in very handy when you want to create beveled buttons from a texture, because a button appearance is created by selectively darkening and lightening the edges of a graphic. Figure 8.19 was created by selecting a portion of the wood texture from Chapter 6.

Figure 8.19

Textured, beveled button created by using masks.

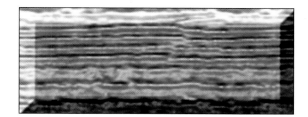

Two masks were used to create the bevel.

The first "new" mask had a 10-pixel–wide white line drawn across the top and down the left side, as in figure 8.20.

After drawing the white lines, notch out the lower left and upper right corners. This can be accomplished quite easily by zooming in and using a combination of the Line and Brush tools.

Once you're satisfied with the bevels, save the mask with Masks, Save, giving it a name such as topleft.msk (catchy, huh?).

Building the second mask is even easier.

Choose Image, Mirror, then Image, Flip—voilà, the second mask (see fig. 8.21)!

With the second mask in place you're ready to add the bevels.

Figure 8.20

Mask for top and left portions of bevel.

Figure 8.21

Mask for bottom and right portions of bevel.

First, shut off the mask editing by choosing Masks, Edit.

Choose Colors, Adjust, Brightness/Contrast and set the %Contrast to 0 and the %Brightness to -30 (These are the values I used for this particular wood texture; you can adjust the numbers to suit your texture.)

Even though, in the preview window of the Brightness/Contrast dialog box, it appears as if the whole image will be affected, only the parts of the image beneath the white portion of the mask will in fact be affected. This will become evident once you click on OK.

If the change is too dark or too light, choose Edit, Undo and reapply the Brightness/ Contrast adjustment, using a different value for %Brightness.

When you're satisfied, choose Masks, Load. You'll be warned that a mask already exists and asked if you want to replace it. Click on Yes and enter the name of the mask you saved in the previous steps.

Choose Colors, Adjust, Brightness/Contrast. This time use a positive number for the %Brightness. I first tried 30 but found it to be too bright, settling on 20 to obtain the effect shown in figure 8.19.

All in all, it wasn't that much work to achieve the realistic textured bevel effect, was it?

Making Selections for Special Effects

Unfortunately, one of the effects that can't be used with a mask in Paint Shop Pro is colorization. One way around this limitation is to use a *selection* rather than a mask to colorize a portion of an image. (There's more about colorization in the "Colorizing Black and White Photos" section later in the chapter.)

Let's say you want to add some glamour to the following black-and-white photo by adding color to the model's lips (see fig. 8.22).

Figure 8.22

"Marianne" photograph by T. Michael Clark.

Tip

Another trick when selecting is to slow down your mouse. Under Windows 95, choose Start, Settings, Control Panel, Mouse, Motion and set the pointer speed to its slowest setting. This will enable you to make more precise movements with the mouse. If you own a Wacom graphics tablet, or a similar tablet that mimics a mouse, this trick will also help you make the fine selections needed for this technique.

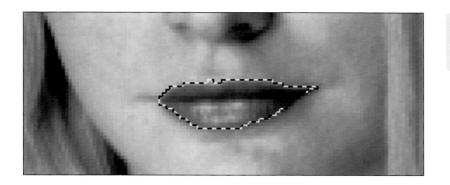

Figure 8.23

Close-up showing selection of model's lips.

Choose the Lasso Selection tool. Zoom in until the area you want to select fills the Paint Shop Pro screen. This will help you make a more perfect selection.

As carefully as you can, draw a selection that contains only the area you want to colorize. In this figure, I've selected the model's lips.

After you've made the initial selection you can fine-tune it by adding to it or subtracting from it. To add to the selection, hold down the Shift key while drawing with the mouse. To subtract from the selection, hold down the CTRL key while drawing with the mouse.

After you've made a selection like the one in the figure 8.23, you'll be ready to apply the color.

Choose Colors, Increase Color Depth, 16.7 Million Colors, first (this was a grayscale image, right?).

Then choose Colors, Adjust, Colorize. I set the Hue to 1 and the Saturation to 80 to get the look in figure 8.24. All set for a magazine (or web zine) lip gloss ad!

Figure 8.24

Final image with color added only to the lips.

Drawing with Selections

Although paint programs are not really meant to be used for drawing or illustrating, there is a technique I use to extend the basic shapes that are available. For this technique to work, the program must be capable of making fairly advanced selections. Fortunately, this is one of the features new to Paint Shop Pro 4.0.

After making a basic selection, you can add to or subtract from the selection. This is accomplished by holding down the Shift key while selecting an area to add or the Ctrl key while selecting an area to subtract. Although this does not give you the flexibility you'd expect from an illustration program, it does provide the opportunity to create some different shapes.

You've already seen some examples of creating different shapes by using this technique in Chapter 4, "Essential Elements of Your Web Page" and again in Chapter 7, "Filters."

Before looking at a more complex example, I want to examine the process in a little more detail.

Say you want an oval button but don't want the standard oval shape. You might want, for instance, to have straight sides on the button.

First, using the Selection tool with the Selection Type set to Ellipse and the Feather to 5, make an oval selection as in figure 8.25.

To create the straight sides, you can cut a rectangular selection from each side.

Set the Selection Type to Rectangle, but before subtracting the rectangle selections, note the x coordinate of the left and right sides of the oval.

Move the cursor to the far left side of the oval and note the first number of the pair of numbers that appears at the bottom left corner of the Paint Shop Pro screen. In the above example I found the x coordinate to be 33. After moving the cursor to the extreme right of the oval, I found the x coordinate of the right side to be 163.

In this example, I decided to cut 30 pixels off of each side. To do this, hold down the Ctrl key and position the cursor above the oval, moving the mouse until the x position reads 63 (33+30=63) Remember to add to the left and subtract from the right.

Hold down the left mouse button and drag down and left until you have a rectangle that cuts off the left end of the oval, as in figure 8.26.

To trim the right side, use 133 (163-30=133) for the x coordinate. Position the cursor above

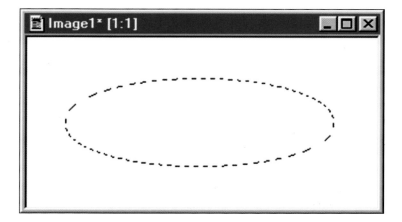

Figure 8.25

Oval selection.

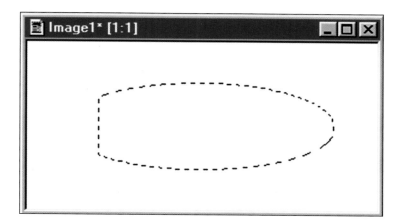

Figure 8.26

Oval selection with straight left side.

the right side of the oval, moving the mouse until the x coordinate equals 133.

Click and hold the left mouse button while dragging down and right until you have a rectangular selection that covers the right end of the oval.

This will leave you with your final shape as in figure 8.27.

After you fill the shape with some color, apply Alien Skin's Inner Bevel filter. Add some text and a drop shadow, and you'll have something resembling the custom button seen in figure 8.28.

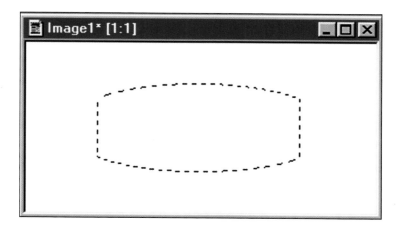

Figure 8.27

Oval selection with straight sides.

Figure 8.28

Straight-sided oval button created by using Selections.

Although I used Adobe's Photoshop to create the GrafX Design logo in figure 8.29, I used essentially the same process.

Figure 8.29

Marble GrafX Design logo.

I started with a circular selection. I then subtracted a long rectangular shape from the center. Keeping the selection type set at rectangle I trimmed out the two areas on the left half to form the stylized G.

This logo started out as a pencil sketch with the idea that it would be drawn by using Selection tools. Keeping the limitations of this technique in mind forced me to come up with an idea that could be easily implemented.

After the G and D shapes were complete, it was a simple matter to fill them with a marble texture, colorize the texture, apply beveled edges, and add the remaining letters of the title by using the Cut-Out filter.

I saved the logo, using Selections, Save, so it's a simple matter to change its look without having to re-create the selection process.

All types of shapes can be created, using the available rectangle, square, circle, and ellipse selection types (for some ideas, look at the buttons in Chapter 7). Let your imagination go and see what you can come up with. Don't forget you can rotate a selection by using Image, Rotate. Have fun!

■Note

The Magic Wand is a very powerful selection tool you should become familiar with. The options for this tool include Match Mode (RGB, Hue and Brightness), Tolerance, and Feather. Usually you'll leave the Match Mode set to RGB and change the value of the Tolerance and Feather as needed. A low Tolerance selects only the same or nearest value color, and a larger value expands the numbers of colors included in the selection. As with the other selection tools, you can add to and subtract from a selection. Learning to use the Magic Wand effectively is something you would definitely benefit from.

Photo Special Effects

Paint Shop Pro might not be quite as powerful as Adobe's Photoshop when it comes to photo manipulation, but there are nevertheless many cool effects you can create by starting out with a photo. The examples speak for themselves. I'll show you how to do things I've never seen done with Paint Shop Pro by anyone else, such as colorizing a black and white photograph, aging a photo, and converting a photo into a sketch.

Colorizing Black-and-White Photos

Colorizing a black-and-white photo can be a long and tedious process even with software as powerful as Photoshop. Admittedly this can be a little more difficult with Paint Shop Pro, but it can be done.

There are a few things to keep in mind when coloring your photos.

▶ Keep the saturation fairly low; otherwise, your photo might end up looking like a movie poster (no problem if that's the look you're going for).

▶ Really spend some time at it, especially with Paint Shop Pro, as you can't use the advanced masking techniques available with higher-end programs.

▶ Always keep a backup, even if this means saving a separate copy after each step. If you make a big enough boo-boo, you'll be glad you can go back a step or two.

▶ Try to pick a photo you think will respond well to the process. When you get halfway through and find out you've already spent three hours at it, it'll be a big help if you're starting to see good results (it's a psychological thing). After a few tries, you'll have a better idea of what to look for.

If the photo is a portrait, start out by colorizing the entire image with a sepia tone, as I did with the image in figure 8.30.

You'll want to play with the Hue and Saturation settings until you get something you like. I can't really give you any hard and fast rules here. Don't expect to come up with extremely realistic skin tones, either, as you'll be somewhat disappointed. Remember, you're colorizing a black and white photo, not creating a color photo.

Figure 8.30

Sepia-tone "colorized" photo of Marianne.

Use the technique outlined in "Making Selections for Special Effects" earlier in this chapter to colorize the lips and eyes. For the lips, I used 1 for the Hue and 80 for the Saturation. For the eyes, I used 174 for the Hue and 30 for the Saturation.

To add to the illusion in the final image, I used the Magic Wand tool to select the background (see fig. 8.31). This was done in several steps by holding down the Shift key to add to the selection.

Figure 8.31

Final colorized black and white photo.

Because Colors, Grayscale doesn't work with a selection, I used Colors, Colorize once again. I left the Hue setting alone but set the Saturation to 0.

Photo Aging and Vignettes

This is a trick I've seen asked about many times, usually in the Photoshop newsgroup on the Usenet. How do you age a photo? In other words, how can you take a portrait and make it look as though it was taken a long time ago?

To "age" a photo, start with the original photo, making sure you have a backup (see fig. 8.32).

If necessary, use Colors, Grayscale to turn the photo into a black-and-white image (see fig. 8.33).

Figure 8.32

"Marianne" photograph by T. Michael Clark.

Figure 8.33

Color photo converted to grayscale.

Then choose Image, Special Filters, Add Noise. In the Add Noise dialog box, select Random and set the value to 20%. You should have something resembling figure 8.34.

Figure 8.34

Noise filter applied to grayscale photo.

Select Image, Rotate and enter Left, Free, and 40 as the options. (The direction really doesn't matter, but this is my way of doing it.)

Then choose Image, Deformations, Wind and set the value to 2.

Rotate the image back by using Image, Rotate with Right, Free, and 40 as the options.

Set the color resolution to 16.7 million by choosing Colors, Increase Color Depth, 16.7 Million Colors.

Choose Colors, Colorize and use 22 for the Hue and 118 for the Saturation. The photo should start to look more aged, as in figure 8.35.

Figure 8.35

Brownish color added to grayscale photo.

Then lighten the photo a little and decrease the contrast to add an even more aged look. Choose Colors, Adjust, Brightness/Contrast and enter 20 and -18 into the %Brightness and %Contrast, respectively (see fig. 8.36).

Set the Feather value to 20. Then, using the Selection tool, crop the photo (see fig. 8.37). Voilà!

Figure 8.36

Photo lightened with contrast lowered.

As an alternative to leaving the photo this way, you can *draw a rectangular selection around the border of the image* and then invert the selection by choosing Selections, Invert. Then use the Retouch tool—set at Smudge, 5, Round, 75% and None—to achieve a vignette-like figure 8.38.

Figure 8.38

Custom border added.

Figure 8.37

Final "aged" photo.

There was a time when photos all came back from the developers with a stylized border such as the one in the previous figure.

For a different vignette, follow all the other steps above until the Retouching. At that point, choose the Selection tool with the Selection Type set to Ellipse and the Feather set to 20.

Draw a selection around the photo. Choose Selections, Invert and press the Delete key. This will set everything inside the selection to the current background color, so you might want to set the background color appropriately. For figure 8.39, I set the background color to black.

Figure 8.39

Aged photo with oval vignette border.

Converting Photos into Drawings

Did you ever wish you could draw somebody's portrait? Well, now you can! This next technique is an easy way to put great versions of family photos on your web site. Or if you're in charge of putting the employees' photos on your web site, this idea will make you the hero of the office.

Start out by preparing the photo. If you have a color photo, change it to black and white. Crop out any unnecessary details. You also might want to get close in, as I did with figure 8.40.

Figure 8.40

Color portrait of Marianne.

Using Colors, Grayscale will convert a color photo to black and white like figure 8.41.

Figure 8.41

Photo converted to black and white.

■ Note

It's hard to say exactly which numbers to use for a particular photo. What you're trying to achieve is a fairly bright, high-contrast image like the one in figure 8.42.

You need to brighten the photo and increase the contrast, as well. You'll do this at least twice with a photo this dark.

Under Colors, Adjust, Brightness/Contrast, I used 20% for the Brightness and 50% for the Contrast. You can see the result in figure 8.42.

Figure 8.42

Brightness and contrast increased.

Click on OK, but you're not there yet, so do the Colors, Adjust, Brightness/Contrast routine again. Figure 8.43 is a much better candidate for the final step in the process.

Figure 8.43

Brightness and contrast increased further.

Here comes the trick that turns this photo into a (well almost) charcoal drawing. Take a look at figure 8.44 for the amazing final result!

Figure 8.44

A pseudo-charcoal drawing.

Choose Image, Edge Filters, Edge Enhance More. What do you think?

If you had some misgivings about what Paint Shop Pro could do, you're probably scratching your head right now in disbelief. You're not alone. I get images e-mailed to me every so often from readers of the GrafX Design online tutorials who've taken my ideas even further than I had imagined. I firmly believe you'll run out of ideas before you can fully discover what Paint Shop Pro is capable of. I've said it before and I'll say it again: *roll up your sleeves and play with this program*. Try different things, use a variety of settings, apply one filter on top of another. The more time you spend exploring the program, the more you'll discover. Most important—have fun!

Chapter 9

Putting It All Together

W ell, this is it! You've got all of the graphical parts of a web site from bullets and backgrounds to text and image maps. It's time to take the plunge and put something together. In this chapter, we'll cover the following:

- ▶ Design Aesthetics
  - ▶ Choosing Your Theme
  - ▶ First Impressions
  - ▶ Following Through
  - ▶ Using an Effective Interface
- ▶ Sample Web Page Themes

Design Aesthetics

This is a tough subject. What looks terrific to one person can look less than appealing to another. One piece of advice I can give you is this: surf, surf, and surf some more. Bookmark the sites that catch your eye, and try to analyze what it is about these sites that appeals to you. While you're at it, examine some sites you don't find pleasing and try to figure out what they're lacking. Eventually you'll get a feeling for what works and what doesn't. Whenever I'm reading through Usenet or answering e-mail and I come across an URL, I click on it to explore the site it points me to. I've found some gems out there, as well as some diamonds in the rough. Sometimes I find a site with some elements that appeal to me as well as some elements that don't. Surfing is hardly ever a waste of time from the webmaster perspective.

If you find a site that appeals to you, don't be afraid to write to the webmaster and ask how a certain look was achieved. Personally, I'm always flattered when someone e-mails me with specific questions about one of my pages or one of my graphics. If you do write to someone, the worst that can happen is that the person will be too busy to answer you. The best is that you can pick up a new technique or two and, maybe, make a new e-mail pal.

The World Wide Web is changing how information is presented to consumers. There are limitless ways to present your ideas to the world. While you're putting your site together, remember one thing—have fun!!! It'll show up in your work, and people will take notice. Keep in mind, as well, that your web site isn't written in stone. Don't be afraid to redo the site completely every once in a while—I do!

Choosing Your Theme

Choosing a theme is one of the first steps in designing your web site. You should take into account the type of audience you're trying to reach. Is your intended audience young or old? Are you trying to reach people with a particular hobby or interest? Questions like these can help you make your choices of colors, fonts, images, or whatever.

Why do you want to put up a web site? Do you have something to share? Maybe you want to talk about your pet(s), or maybe you're an amateur photographer who wants to show off some of your best work. Whatever your reason, you should have a theme for your site.

First Impressions

Your home page is like a first impression. Even if readers later bookmark some other page on your site, the home page is where most of them will first meet you. I feel it's important to make a good first impression. I'll sometimes mark a site to go back and explore, based solely on the merits of the home page. On the other hand, I'll not bother exploring a site further if the home page doesn't appeal to me.

You should try to get your web site's message across on the home page. Try to do so without causing the reader to wait too long. People can get impatient waiting for large graphic logos and dozens of buttons to load.

A home page serves much the same function as the cover of a magazine. Will surfers want to browse through your site or go on to the next one?

Try to give readers a clue, either visually or literally, as to what they can expect at your site. Entice them if you can. I've been to sites where the home page contains nothing more than an image with a link into the site. Some of these I followed and some I didn't. You won't be able to please everyone, but if you hit your intended audience, you'll know you're doing something right.

Following Through

Okay, you got the reader to go past the home page into your site, now what? Keep them interested! Try not to go off on bizarre tangents (unless that's what your site is all about). Personally, I dislike clicking on a link and ending up on a page that seems totally out of character with the rest of the site. (Kind of like what a detergent ad does to a good black and white murder mystery.)

Test your links. Make sure your images do, in fact, load. Get a friend to log onto your site and check it out. If you can, visit it yourself with different systems from different locations. I sometimes go to one of the Internet cybercafes and check out my site from there to see what it looks like on a different system. You might be surprised at what you see.

If you have several topics or hobbies you'd like to show off on the web, consider building separate sites for them. You can always find a way to link them together that doesn't detract from either.

Using an Effective Interface

What makes up an effective interface is another one of those tough questions, like what makes an image a button.

Should you use many small buttons or an image map? How will you provide clues to your readers about where they are within your web site? Is it easy to navigate through your site?

I become intensely irritated when I happen upon a beautifully done site and abruptly find myself on a page that doesn't link directly back to any other pages on the site. Of course, there's always the Back button on the browser, but it's really not intended for that purpose. What I'm trying to say is that you should provide your readers with a graceful way to move from page to page and, usually, a way to get back to the home page or at least to some other major road mark.

How you go about building the interface and which components you use is all part of the fun (and sometimes the pain) of designing and creating a web site. If you think your ego can handle it, you can always post to a newsgroup or two and invite people to stop by and critique your site. Some newsgroups to try are *comp.graphics.misc* and *comp.infosystems.www.authoring.images*. Of course, if your web site has information of interest to a specific audience, you could try asking the readers of a newsgroup with a similar topic to stop by and visit your site. For example, if your web site discusses exotic cats, you might try the *rec.pets.cats* group. Before you post on any of these newsgroups, though, read through them to get a feel for whether this type of request would be appropriate. Read through the Frequently Asked Questions (FAQ), as well, to see if it's acceptable to post this sort of message.

Sample Web Page Themes

Using one of the images from Chapter 6, "Backgrounds and Borders," and some of the techniques described in various other parts of the book, let's look at putting together a sample page.

Let's say this fictitious page would be of interest to teens. I'll call it the "Hole in the Wall" web site. Remember the only matter of interest, as far as this book is concerned, is the quality and appropriateness of the graphics. I'm not going to get into the underlying HTML or what the possible content would be.

Figure 9.1 is similar to figure 6.41. I'll be using it for a border.

Figure 9.1

Brick edge border effect.

Using the technique described in Chapter 6, I've made this image tile vertically so it can be used for an edge border. Using the same border on all the pages at a specific site is a good way to rest assured your readers won't all of a sudden feel as though they've wandered into the twilight zone after clicking on a link.

To create the logo/title for this page, I drew a selection that looked something like a hole in a plaster wall. With the selection active, I drew inside the selection, using the same techniques I used to create the brick border. I applied Hot

Wax as well, and before removing the selection, I ran the Alien Skin Cut-Out filter to add a drop shadow inside the hole.

Because I wanted this site to appeal to a younger audience, I chose an informal font for the title.

Figure 9.2 is the finished title image.

Figure 9.2

Hole in the Wall title logo.

For fun I colored the letters by using the same method I used for the bricks.

To get an idea of what this page would look like, I quickly put it together, using Homesite 2.0, and viewed it with MSIE (Microsoft Internet Explorer). You can see what it looks like in figure 9.3.

In keeping with the street corner nature of this site, the navigational buttons might resemble figure 9.4.

Figure 9.3

Screen capture of the fictitious "Hole in the Wall" web site.

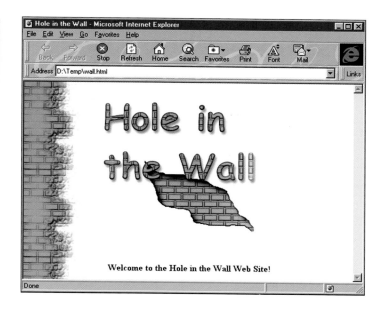

Figure 9.4

Buttons for Hole in the Wall web site.

Notice, too, how I've kept the same font throughout.

With the addition of a bulleted list of topics viewers could expect to see here, and perhaps an e-mail link to the webmaster, this home page would be ready to go.

The next example, a live Netscape screen capture, shows the current incarnation of the GrafX Design web site (http://www.grafx-design.com). It sports a quick-loading imagemap and includes a text version of the

links for those surfers who turn off their browser's graphics capabilities (see fig. 9.5). It's sometimes hard to say why I come up with a specific design. I doodle a lot, keep some, and throw out many more. Again, just try things until they work.

If you load this home page into your browser, you'll see another small logo to show you which page you are on, a couple of short paragraphs about the site, the copyright notice, and an e-mail link to the webmaster.

Figure 9.5

Screen capture of the
GrafX Design web site.

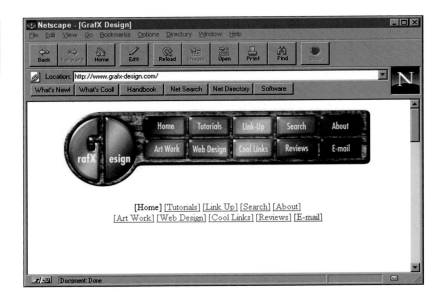

Simple, yet—I hope—effective. So far I've received only positive responses (and a job offer or two).

I'd have to say that, when it comes to web design, you're only limited by your imagination. Okay, so HTML is somewhat limiting, and so is the current state of web browsers, but a lot can be done, even with the current technology.

Get out there, surf around, see what others have done, and have fun building your own piece of virtual space.

Author's Note

I'd like to take this chance to tell you how much fun I've had putting this book together. I hope that it has given you many ideas of what can be done with Paint Shop Pro, and that after going through the tutorials you'll take my ideas even further. I'm absolutely certain that with a bit of work (but less than you ever thought!) you will be able to develop some truly stunning and original web artwork. To that end, I hope the next time I'm out there surfing the web I will come across a page you've built by using the techniques I've described here. I also hope you've found ways to stretch the limits of your software and your imagination.

Happy web designing,

J. Michael Clark

Appendix

Resources on the Internet

This list is not complete by any means but rather a starting point. There are literally thousands of references on the Internet, waiting for you to find them and explore.

Usenet Newsgroups

- ▶ comp.graphics
- ▶ comp.graphics.misc
- ▶ alt.graphics
- ▶ alt.design.graphics
- ▶ comp.graphics.apps.photoshop
- ▶ comp.infosystems.web.authoring.images
- ▶ alt.fractal-design.painter
- ▶ alt.corel.graphics
- ▶ alt.graphics.pixutils

Web Sites

- ▶ **GrafX Design** www.grafx-design.com
  This is my site.

- ▶ **Alien Skin Software** www.alienskin.com
  Plug-in filters.

- ▶ **Metatools, Inc.** www.metatools.com
  Plug-in filters.

- ▶ **The Flux Collection**
  www.dsb.com/products/dsbflux.html
  More plug-in filters.

- ▶ **HomeSite HTML editor**
  www.dexnet.com/homesite.html
  Great WYSIWYG HTML editor.

- ▶ **Learn good design by looking at bad design** www.webpagesthatsuck.com
  Great advice on what NOT to do on your web site.

- ▶ **JASC Inc Software** www.jasc.com
  The creators of Paint Shop Pro.

- ▶ **Adobe Systems, Inc.** www.adobe.com
  Photoshop's creators.

- ▶ **Fractal Design Online** www.fractal.com
  Painter's creators.

- ▶ **Corel Corporation** www.corel.com
  Creators of CorelDRAW!

Some Good References about Images and the Web

- ▶ **World Wide Web FAQ**
  www.boutell.com/faq/

- ▶ **Preparing Graphics for the Web**
  www.servtech.com/public/dougg/
  graphics/index.html

- ▶ **Optimizing Web Graphics**
  www.webreference.com/dev/graphics/

- ▶ **GIF? JPEG? Which should you use?**
  www.adobe.com/studio/tipstechniques/
  GIFJPGchart/main.html

- ▶ **The Browser Safe Palette**
  www.the-light.com/netcol.html

- ▶ **JPEG FAQ**
  www.landfield.com/faqs/jpeg-faq/

- ▶ **Poynton's Color Technology Page**
  www.inforamp.net/~poynton/Poynton-
  colour.html

- ▶ **Scanning Photos for the Web**
  www.photo.net/philg/how-to-scan-
  photos.html

Search Engines

- ▶ **AltaVista** www.altavista.com

- ▶ **Yahoo!** www.yahoo.com

Freeware and Shareware

- ▶ **The Ultimate Collection of Winsock Software** www.tucows.com

- ▶ **Shareware search engine**
  www.shareware.com

Index

Symbols

dithering

G

gamma, defined, 20, 148
gamma corrections, setting options, 148
Gamma Correction option, 110
geometric tiles, 146
GIF (Graphical Interchange Format), 47-49
  advantages/disadvantages, 37
  colors, 36-37
    transparent, 52
  files, saving, 82
  images, transparent, 190-194
  interlacing, 52-53
  transparent, creating, 190-194
GIF?/JPEG? Web site, 226
Glass filter, 178
Glow filter, 178
gold text, 99-103
  color, deepening, 102
Gradient Fill Direction dialog box, 94, 149, 201
  setting options, 82, 100-101
gradient tiles, 149-151
graffiti text, 124-125
  advanced, 126-127
GrafX Design Web site, 56, 104, 195, 221-222, 225
Graphical User Interface (GUI), 78
graphics
  color depth, 51
  compression, 51
  cursor, placing in center, 138
  dithering, 29-30
  edges
    artifacts, 48
    feathering, 46-48
  files
    converting, 38-39
    GIF, 47-49
    JPG, 47-50
    manipulating, 38-39
    saving, 101, 140-141
  grayscale, converting from
   color photo, 143

  jaggies, antialiasing, 43-46
  masks, 200-202
  saving, 70, 74-75
  selections
    adding to, 205
    drawing with, 205-208
    rotating, 208
  uncompressed, memory used, 41
grayscale, color photo, converting from, 143
Grayscale command (Colors menu), 82, 143, 148-149, 210
  Gamma Correction option, 110
GUI (Graphical User Interface), 78

H

Hand tool, functions, 17
Help menu, functions, 16
highlights, text, raised, 114-115
Hole in the Wall sample Web site, 220-221
Home button, x and y coordinates, 197
HomeSite HTML editor Web site, 226
Hot Wax Coating option, 105, 113, 118
hot wax coatings, textures, 158
Hot Wax filter, 168-169
Hot Wax option, 102-103
HSB (Hue, Saturation, Brightness) Noise filter, 27, 179-180
HTML
  codes
    "commenting out," 196-197
    imagemaps, forming, 196
  HomeSite HTML editor Web site, 226
  imagemaps, 195
  lists
    implementing, 56
    numbered, 57
  tags
    <AREA>, 199-200
    <IMG>, 199
    <MAP>, 196
  Teach Yourself Web Publishing with HTML 3.0, 196

I

icons
  navigation, creating, 78-79
  text, combining, 79
  Web pages, space saving, 78

Image masks
  images
    adding, 97
    editing, 98
  text, 93-95

Image menu, functions, 16

Image menu commands
  Add Borders, 83
  Crop, 41
  Deformations, 61
    setting options, 96, 211
    Skew option, setting options, 92
  Edge Filters, Edge Enhance
  More option, 215
  Flip, 96
  Mirror, setting options, 203
  Normal Filters, 65, 90, 103, 153, 179
    Blur More filter, 75, 77, 84, 202
    setting options, 95, 98, 105, 123
    Soften More filter, 81
  Paste, setting options, 133
  Plug-In Filters, 181, 187
    setting options, 186
  Resample, setting options, 121
  Rotate, 129, 132, 208
    setting options, 111, 211
  Special Effects, 102-103, 164, 168, 170
    Add Drop Shadow option, 81, 83-84, 92
    setting options, 105, 111-114, 117-119,
    125, 130, 152, 165, 173, 175
  Special Filters, 147
    Add Noise filter, 83, 211
    setting options, 109

imagemaps, 194-197
  button bars, creating as, 198-200
  buttons, comparing, 197-198

HTML codes, 195-197
  x and y coordinates, locating, 197

images
  compression, lossy versus lossless, 50-51
  cropping, 40-41
  displayed with GIF interlacing, 52-53
  displayed with JPG progressive, 52-53
  enlarging, 41-46
  extruding, 106-108
  gamma, 20
  interpolation, 39-40
  jaggies, 44-45
  layers, adding, 108
  lossy format, 37
  masks
    adding, 97
    editing, 98
  pixelation, 42
  pixels, 44-45
  resampling, 39-40
  resizing, 39-40
  rotating, 111
  saving, 37
  selecting, 105
  text, fitting into, 121
  tile patterns, filling, 142
  tiling, testing possibility of, 144
  transparent, GIF format, 190-194

Images menu commands, Special Effects, 73

<IMG> tag, 199

Increase Color Depth command (Colors
menu), 45, 111, 152
  setting options, 205

Inner Bevel filter, 177, 180-181, 207
  plastic effects, 182
  setting options, 182

interfaces, Web sites, 219

interlacing, GIF, 52-53

Internet
  fonts, availability of, 89
  resources, 225-226
  Usenet Newsgroups, 225
  Web sites, 225-226

interpolation, images, 39-40
Invert command (Selections menu), 75, 97, 103, 105, 119, 128, 130, 154, 212
   Feather option, 73

J

jaggies
   antialiasing, 23
   images, 44
   text, removing, 92
JASC Inc. Software Web site, 226
JASC Inc. Web site, 152
JPEG (Joint Photographic Experts Group), 36-37, 47-50
   advantages/disadvantages, 38
   compression, lossy versus lossless, 50-51
   graphics, 48-51
   lossy format, 37
   progression, 52-53
JPEG FAQ Web site, 226
JPG, *see* JPEG

K-L

keyboard shortcuts, location of, 90

Lasso Selection tool, 205
   setting options, 63-64
Lasso tool, functions, 17
layers, 3D text, adding, 108
Learn good design by looking at bad design Web site, 226
Line tool, 80, 122
   functions, 18
   setting options, 68
Linear Gradient, Fill tool, 100
Linear Gradient mask, text, blurring, 202
Linear Gradient option, Fill tool, 71
Linear Gradient Options dialog box, 72
links, Web sites, testing, 219
Load command (Selections menu), 125
Load Palette command (Colors menu), 31

logos
   backgrounds, 141-142
   fonts, choosing, 88-89
   saving, 208
   text
      3D, 106-109
      beveled, 117-119
      chrome, 103-105
      circles, in, 127-131
      embossed, 109-112
      gold, 99-103
      graffiti, 124-127
      opacity effects, 131-133
      raised, 112-114
      raised, shadows/highlights, 114-115
      raised, textures, 116-117
      reflective, 98-99
      see-through, 120-122
      shadowed, 90-92
      shadowed, foreshadowing, 95-98
      shadowed, variations, 93-95
      spray (neon effect), 123-124
lossy, compression, 37, 48-51

M

Magic Wand tool, 73, 101, 152
   beveled text, 119
   functions, 17
   options, 208
   setting options, 99-100, 103, 128, 130
   Tolerance option, 60
<MAP> tag, 196
marbled textures, 84
marquee, 108
Mask menu commands, Save, 203
masks
   buttons, beveled, 203-205
   graphics, 201-202
   grayscale, functions, 200-201
   image masks, 93-95
   saving, 203

Paint Shop Pro 4.x window

X-Z